CANDLELIGHT

CLASSICS

Gourmet Cuisine in Minutes
from Chef's Signature

BENJAMIN

On the cover: Sea Scallops in White Wine Sauce (page 90), Asparagus with Lemon Sauce (page 99)

Photography by Charles Masters

Printed and bound in the United States of America

Shrimp fork pg. 14, platter and plate pg. 75, bowls pg. 94, plates pg. 115 courtesy of Baccarat. Platter pg. 84 courtesy of Pierre Deux. Special thanks to Country Gear.

Library of Congress Catalog Card Number: 86-71539

ISBN: 0-87502-195-6

Published and Produced by The Benjamin Company, Inc.
                                    One Westchester Plaza
                                    Elmsford, New York 10523

First printing: August 1986

Contents

Introduction

Congratulations! You have selected a cookware collection so distinctive in its attractiveness and performance quality that it has earned the coveted prize of chefs' endorsements. Now you can exercise your culinary talents to the fullest, confident in the knowledge that Chef's Signature™ Cookware has been meticulously designed and elegantly crafted to complement and enhance your gourmet flair.

While there are dozens of excellent cookware lines on the market, *our* dream was to make a detailed examination of all those pots and pans and — selecting only the finest features of each — create the *ultimate* cookware. Our search led us to one of Europe's foremost manufacturers of professional cookware. The manufacturer, drawing on the expertise gained through years of creating cookware for gourmet chefs from some of the world's most renowned clubs and restaurants, came up with an original design of uncommon beauty and unparalleled quality. Finally, under the most exacting standards of painstaking craftsmanship, that unique design was brought to life as Chef's Signature Cookware, created exclusively for our customers, and presented to you, with pride, by Amway.

The Inside Story

Chef's Signature Cookware is crafted from solid spun aluminum, the most efficient heat conductor of all affordable metals. Aluminum construction allows heat to spread quickly and evenly over the entire pan surface, eliminating "hot spots" to help prevent scorching.

The handsome pewter-look surface of Chef's Signature is not simply an outer coating but is actually a part of the metal itself. Through a complex electro-chemical process called anodization, the surface of the cookware undergoes a permanent internal alteration, resulting in a hard protective coating that won't crack, peel, or chip even when metal utensils are used.

The handles on all Chef's Signature pans are crafted from heavy-duty cast-iron. That means that your cookware can safely be used both on the stovetop and in the oven for convenient, one-pan cooking. (Handles do get hot, so remember to use a potholder or oven mitt.) Layers of copper and nickel plating provide the attractive, even finish, and handles are secured with three anodized aluminum rivets for solid durability.

Chef's Signature has been approved by the National Sanitation Foundation (NSF) as a commercial-quality cookware. Its gleaming brushed stainless steel lids are designed to fit snugly for the most efficient steaming and slow-simmering. Special "bumpers" — the added thickness at the top and bottom of the saucepans and Dutch oven — add stability to the pan configuration.

Inside and out, Chef's Signature combines exquisite styling with ultimate functionality, for a cookware of heirloom quality that you'll be proud to show off to family and friends.

What It Does Best

Gourmet chefs have long known that, whether they're preparing a sauce or a soufflé, perfect results depend on something more than the right ingredients and culinary know-how. That hidden something is the quality of their skillet or saucepan, the factor that can make the difference between a watery disaster and a masterpiece.

The superior quality of Chef's Signature shows in its superbly even heat distribution, which eliminates hot spots so puddings, candy, eggs, and sauces are less likely to stick or scorch. Soups, bisques, and stews don't take quite so long to simmer to perfection, either — surrounded by steady, even heat their flavors blend and mellow beautifully. And heatproof versatility lets you start a side dish or entrée on the stovetop and finish baking, crisping, or browning it inside the oven, without taking the time and trouble to switch pans.

Once you've put Chef's Signature to the test in your own kitchen, you'll be amazed at its versatility and at the splendid results. Here are just a few ideas to introduce you to each pan's special talents and applications.

5.5-quart Dutch oven: Perfect for searing, then simmering or ovenbaking roasts; cooking soups, stews, bisques, lobster, casseroles, pasta, preserves, hot drinks.

2.7-quart, 1.8-quart, 1-quart saucepans: Cooking sauces, chili, fondue, candy, puddings, dips, rice; heating canned foods; steaming fresh or heating frozen vegetables; melting butter and chocolate.

9-inch gourmet frying pan: Browning or panfrying ground beef, sandwiches, bacon, eggs; ovenbaked pan pizza; ovenbaked quiches; omelets, French toast, crêpes, pancakes; stir-frying. The Dutch oven lid is designed to fit the gourmet frying pan as well, making it perfect for sautéing chops, vegetables; panfrying or poaching fish, shellfish, chicken; panbaking soufflés.

Cooking Hints

With the help of these few sensible precautions and an insider's look at a few of our chefs' culinary secrets, you'll soon be turning out effortless omelets, elegant sauces, meat masterpieces, and vegetables that snap with natural color and flavor.

EGGS are delicate, and high heat in any pan can make them rubbery and tough. Chef's Signature's even heat distribution lets you cook perfect eggs on low and medium heat settings. For *scrambled eggs,* cook in the gourmet frying pan over medium-low to medium heat for a creamy, soft texture. For *hard-cooked eggs,* start eggs in cold water in the 3-quart saucepan; bring water just to a boil over medium heat, then reduce heat and simmer about 10 minutes. Remove from heat and plunge eggs in cold water. *Fry eggs* in melted butter, bacon fat, or vegetable oil in the gourmet frying pan over medium heat until both whites and yolks are set.

SAUCES can scorch, curdle, or overcook over high heat. Use low or medium heat settings for even cooking of glazes for meat, white sauce or butter sauces, gravies, and dessert sauces. Stir gravies occasionally; stir dessert sauces constantly for even consistency.

MEAT can be seared quickly in the gourmet frying pan or Dutch oven over medium to medium-high heat to seal in the juices; reduce heat to low and cook, simmer, or braise until tender. Roasts may be seared in the Dutch oven and then ovenbaked in the same pan, along with herbs and vegetables.

VEGETABLES may be cooked or steamed in a very small amount of water in Chef's Signature to preserve nutrients. Clean and rinse fresh vegetables; cook frozen vegetables without added water. Potatoes are the exception: they should be covered with water for even cooking. Place vegetables in the saucepans or Dutch oven, cover, and cook over medium heat until tender-crisp. Cook in butter and herbs for added flavor. *Stir-fry* vegetables in the gourmet frying pan over medium heat. Cut on the diagonal to expose more surface for faster cooking.

Care and Cleaning

The anodized aluminum surface of Chef's Signature makes using and caring for your cookware simple and trouble-free. No special preparation steps are needed — just wash pans in hot, mild suds before using for the first time, and then rinse and towel dry.

You can use plastic, wood, rubber, and even metal utensils without fear of damaging the cookware surface, but, as with any fine cookware, you should not cut or chop foods inside the pans with sharp-edged tools or knives.

Because of Chef's Signature's excellent heat conductivity, you'll find that most cooking can be accomplished on moderate or low heat. Prolonged cooking at extremely high temperatures not only wastes energy but can cause food to stick or burn.

To keep your pans looking like new, wash them in hot, sudsy water (Dish Drops® Dishwashing Liquid or a similar mild detergent) after each use. Never subject your cookware to the harsh detergents and extreme temperatures of a dishwasher, and never use your pans to store foods with high acid or salt content — in time, cookware can become stained or pitted from the interaction of its natural elements with the elements in those foods.

For mineral stains or discoloration, scour pans and lids with a stainless steel pad (an Amway Scrub Bud® Scouring Sponge is perfect). Stubborn stains may be removed by applying a paste of water and a mild abrasive cleanser like Amway Chrome and Glass Heavy Duty Cleaner. Gently rub, rinse, and then wash and towel dry. For burned-on food, fill the cooled pan with cold water, bring to a boil, and simmer until the food loosens. Empty the pan, and wash when cool.

Warranty/Guarantee

Chef's Signature Cookware comes with a three-year warranty that is your assurance of superb materials and craftsmanship. Above and beyond that warranty you have the Satisfaction Guarantee that comes with every Amway product. Your complete satisfaction is guaranteed with Chef's Signature Cookware — or your money back!

About the Recipes

From appetizers, soups, sandwiches, and side dishes to entrées, sauces, desserts, and candy, you'll soon be preparing quick snacks and elegant, full-course meals in less time and with greater ease than you ever imagined possible.

The superior performance and stovetop-to-oven flexibility of Chef's Signature Cookware allow us to bring you an array of recipes that are unusually quick and easy. In fact, few of the over 130 recipes that follow take longer than 30 minutes to prepare. Yet, whether you're serving up cornbread or vichyssoise, each dish has the excellent appearance, texture, and taste, and the special touch of originality that distinguish true gourmet cuisine.

You'll also find wonderful menus in the following chapters, menus that combine selected recipes to create culinary events as homey as Sunday Brunch or as elegant as After-the-Concert Dessert & Coffee. And a Special Section brings you recipes expressly created by the chefs at Amway's Better LifePlans Institute, where naturally healthful foods are the star of many envied dining experiences and the start of a life-enriching diet.

It is our hope that this collection of recipes will give you just a taste of the wonderful versatility and performance expertise of your cookware. So don your chef's hat, tie on your apron, and get ready to cook with confidence. You're far from alone in the kitchen, because you hold years of culinary experience in your hands — you're cooking with Chef's Signature, developed in France for you . . . and all the other gourmet chefs of the world.

Chef Dan Hugelier

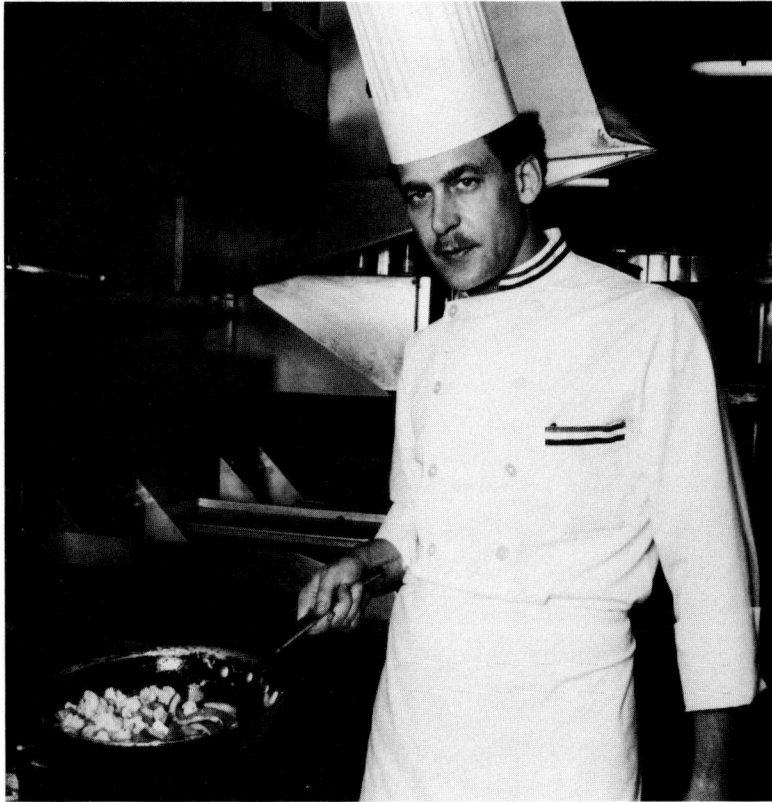

Executive Chef at the Amway Grand Plaza Hotel, Chef Dan Hugelier placed first in the 1986 Culinary Olympics in Detroit, Michigan, and the Great Lakes Food Show. Chef Dan, who is Team Captain of the USA Culinary Olympics Team, will soon compete in Singapore as part of the Food & Hotel Asia '86 — the 5th Salon Culinaire.

"It's easy to produce quality when you start with it. That's why I'm so pleased to have available a line of cooking utensils that incorporates all the finest features of continental cookware. The exceptional performance reliability of Chef's Signature frees me to concentrate on the personal artistry that is at the heart of all creative cuisine."

Chef Gilles Renusson

Executive Pastry Chef at the AAA Four Diamond Amway Grand Plaza Hotel, Chef Gilles Renusson received a first-place gold medal for exceptional creativeness in the Detroit Culinary Olympics and the Great Lakes Food Show of April 1986.

"Finally, a pan in the U.S. that matches European copper. Both in appearance and performance, Chef's Signature is the long-awaited answer to expensive European cookware. No hot spots, no scorched sauces — cooking with these pans is truly a pleasure."

Chef Mike Green

Garde-Manger at the world-class Grand Plaza, Chef Mike Green was recently awarded a silver medal for outstanding performance in the Detroit, Michigan, Culinary Olympics and the Great Lakes Food Show of 1986.

"People who expect the best use the best. That means nothing but the finest, freshest ingredients go into fine gourmet cuisine — and you don't put perfect food into less-than-perfect pans. Chef's Signature is the kind of cookware one may use with confidence, because it always lives up to the expectations of those who will make no compromises with quality."

Marinated Shrimp (page 16)

Chapter One

Entertaining
Hors d'Oeuvre

MARINATED SHRIMP

½ cup olive oil
1 tablespoon lemon juice
1 teaspoon Worcestershire sauce
1 teaspoon soy sauce
1 teaspoon Italian seasoning
½ teaspoon basil
½ teaspoon chervil
1 pound medium-size shrimp, shelled and deveined,
tails intact
2 tablespoons butter or margarine, divided
Chervil or parsley sprigs for garnish
Cocktail sauce to serve

Combine oil, lemon juice, Worcestershire, soy sauce, Italian seasoning, basil, and chervil in shallow glass dish. Stir until blended. Add shrimp and stir until coated. Cover and refrigerate 4 to 6 hours, stirring occasionally.

Melt 1 tablespoon butter in gourmet frying pan. Drain shrimp and add half the shrimp to pan. Cook over medium heat just until pink. Arrange on warm serving platter and cover with aluminum foil to keep warm. Repeat with remaining 1 tablespoon butter and shrimp. Garnish with chervil and serve with cocktail sauce.

4 to 6 servings   *(See photo page 14)*

CHEDDAR AND WINE FONDUE

⅓ cup all-purpose flour
⅛ teaspoon nutmeg
⅛ teaspoon salt
4 cups (1 pound) cubed Cheddar cheese
1 cup apple juice
1 cup dry white wine
French bread, cubed, and apple wedges to serve

Combine flour, nutmeg, and salt in large bowl. Add cheese and toss to coat. Set aside.

Heat apple juice and wine in 3-quart saucepan over medium heat. Add cheese mixture, ½ cup at a time, stirring constantly as cheese melts. Reduce heat to low and cook until thickened, stirring constantly.

Pour into fondue pot. Provide long-handled fondue forks to dip bread cubes and apple wedges into fondue.

4 to 6 servings

ITALIAN CHEESE FONDUE

½ pound lean ground beef
½ pound sweet Italian sausage, crumbled
1 medium-size onion, chopped
1 clove garlic, minced
2 teaspoons Italian seasoning
2 teaspoons brown sugar
1 teaspoon Worcestershire sauce
1 teaspoon salt
½ teaspoon freshly ground pepper
1 jar (15½ ounces) spaghetti sauce
½ cup dry red wine
2 cups (8 ounces) grated mozzarella cheese
1 cup (4 ounces) grated Cheddar cheese
1 loaf Italian bread, cubed, to serve

Brown beef and sausage in Dutch oven over medium heat. Drain off excess fat. Add onion and garlic and cook until onion is transparent. Add Italian seasoning, brown sugar, Worcestershire, salt, and pepper. Stir until well mixed.

Stir spaghetti sauce and wine into meat mixture. Cover and cook until hot and bubbly. Reduce heat to medium-low. Add mozzarella and Cheddar cheeses and stir until melted. Pour into fondue pot. Provide long-handled fondue forks to dip bread in fondue.

about 4 cups

Crab Meat Fondue Française

CRAB MEAT FONDUE FRANÇAISE

2 tablespoons all-purpose flour
1 tablespoon chopped fresh parsley
¼ teaspoon salt
¼ teaspoon white pepper
3 cups (12 ounces) shredded Swiss cheese
¾ cup dry white wine
1 clove garlic
1 package (6 ounces) frozen crab meat,
thawed and drained, divided
1 tablespoon kirsch
1 loaf French bread, cubed, to serve

Combine flour, parsley, salt, and white pepper in large bowl. Add cheese and toss until coated. Set aside.

Heat wine and garlic in 3-quart saucepan over medium heat until wine just comes to a boil. Remove garlic. Reduce heat to low and add floured cheese, ½ cup at a time, until melted, stirring constantly.

Set aside 2 to 3 tablespoons crab meat for garnish. Add remaining crab meat to fondue and cook until heated through. Remove from heat and stir in kirsch.

Pour into fondue pot. Top with reserved crab meat. Provide long-handled fondue forks to dip bread in fondue.

about 3 cups

COCKTAIL SPARERIBS

1 teaspoon cornstarch
¼ cup ketchup
1 tablespoon soy sauce
2 tablespoons molasses
1 teaspoon Worcestershire sauce
1 clove garlic, minced
2 pounds pork loin back ribs, cut in 2-inch pieces
¼ cup vegetable oil

Dissolve cornstarch in 2 tablespoons water. Stir until smooth. Combine ketchup, soy sauce, molasses, Worcestershire, and garlic in shallow dish. Stir in cornstarch mixture. Add ribs and turn to coat both sides. Cover and refrigerate at least 4 hours, turning ribs occasionally.

Heat oil in gourmet frying pan over medium-high heat. Drain ribs and add to pan, a few at a time. Cook until brown and crispy. Place cooked ribs in Dutch oven, cover, and keep warm over low heat. Repeat with remaining ribs.

Serve hot as finger food.

about 40 ribs

CUCUMBER CANAPÉS

2 large cucumbers
½ pound ground pork
2 tablespoons soy sauce
1 tablespoon dry sherry
1 teaspoon sugar
½ teaspoon ginger
Salt to taste
¼ teaspoon lemon pepper
2 tablespoons peanut or vegetable oil

Peel cucumbers and cut in 2-inch circles. Scoop out seeds from center of each circle. Set cucumbers aside.

Brown pork in gourmet frying pan over medium heat. Remove from heat and drain off excess fat. Add soy sauce, sherry, sugar, ginger, salt, and lemon pepper to pan. Stir until well mixed. Divide pork mixture evenly and fill hole in each cucumber circle.

Increase heat to medium-high and heat oil. Fry stuffed cucumber circles until crisp, turning to brown evenly on both sides. Reduce heat to medium-low and cook until cucumbers are tender. Remove with slotted spoon.

8 appetizers

CHINESE CHICKEN WINGS

8 chicken wings (about 1 pound)
⅓ cup soy sauce
¼ cup firmly packed brown sugar
2 tablespoons barbecue sauce
2 tablespoons dry sherry
1 teaspoon ginger
1 clove garlic, minced
Hot pepper sauce to taste
1 tablespoon butter or margarine
1 tablespoon vegetable oil
Green onions for garnish

Cut off wing tips. Cut chicken wings in half through joint. Place soy sauce, brown sugar, barbecue sauce, sherry, ginger, garlic, and hot pepper sauce in medium-size bowl. Mix until well blended. Arrange chicken wings in single layer in shallow glass baking dish. Pour marinade over wings and turn to coat. Cover and refrigerate several hours, turning occasionally. Drain chicken wings, reserving marinade.

Heat butter and oil in gourmet frying pan and cook wings over medium heat until nicely browned and tender, basting with reserved marinade several times. Serve hot as appetizer, garnished with decoratively trimmed green onions, or with rice for light meal.

16 appetizers *(See photo page 25)*

CHEF'S-SECRET DEVILED EGGS

4 hard-cooked eggs
2 to 4 tablespoons mayonnaise
1 tablespoon finely chopped onion
1 tablespoon chopped fresh parsley
¼ teaspoon prepared mustard
Salt and freshly ground pepper to taste
2 tablespoons butter or margarine
Dijon-style mustard to serve

Cut eggs in half crosswise and remove yolks. Set whites aside.
Mash yolks with fork in small bowl. Add mayonnaise, onion,
parsley, mustard, salt, and pepper. Stir until well mixed. Spoon
yolk mixture into egg white halves and smooth with knife.

Melt butter in gourmet frying pan over medium heat. Place
eggs in butter, stuffed-side down, and fry until lightly browned.
Turn eggs over and fry quickly until just heated through.

Serve with mustard.

4 servings

PARTY RUMAKI

½ cup soy sauce
1 clove garlic, minced
1½ pounds bacon
1 can (8 ounces) pineapple chunks, drained
1 can (6 ounces) whole water chestnuts, drained
25 stuffed green olives

Combine soy sauce and garlic in small bowl. Set aside.

Cut bacon slices in half. Place 1 pineapple chunk on each half-
slice bacon. Roll up and fasten with wooden toothpick. Repeat
with remaining pineapple, water chestnuts, and olives. Place
rumaki in shallow dish and brush soy sauce mixture on each
piece. Turn over and brush with remaining soy sauce mixture.
Cover and refrigerate 1 hour.

Preheat gourmet frying pan. Add rumaki, a few at a time, and
fry, turning pieces over, until brown and crispy. Remove from
pan and drain on paper towels. Repeat with remaining rumaki.

about 66 rumaki

TINY MEATBALLS IN CURRANT GLAZE

MEATBALLS
2 pounds lean ground beef
2 eggs, beaten
1 medium-size onion, finely chopped
¼ cup dry bread crumbs
¼ cup light cream
½ teaspoon Italian seasoning
½ teaspoon salt
¼ teaspoon freshly ground pepper
2 tablespoons vegetable oil

GLAZE
2 tablespoons butter or margarine
1 small onion, finely chopped
1 clove garlic, minced
1 jar (12 ounces) currant jelly
1 bottle (12 ounces) chili sauce
1 teaspoon Worcestershire sauce
1 envelope (1¼ ounces) brown gravy mix

To prepare meatballs, place beef, eggs, onion, bread crumbs, cream, Italian seasoning, salt, and pepper in medium-size bowl. Mix well and shape into 1-inch balls. Heat oil in gourmet frying pan over medium heat. Add meatballs in 2 batches and cook until browned on all sides. Remove meatballs with slotted spoon and place in heated chafing dish. Cover and set aside.

To prepare glaze, melt butter in 3-quart saucepan over medium heat. Add onion and garlic and sauté until onion is transparent. Add jelly, chili sauce, Worcestershire, and gravy mix, and stir well. Reduce heat to low and bring to a boil. Pour hot sauce over meatballs and serve with cocktail picks.

36 meatballs

Menu:
Party Appetizers for Ten

Tangy Crab Meat Dip (page 27)
crudités and crackers
Cheddar and Wine Fondue (page 16)
French bread cubes
Tiny Meatballs in Currant Glaze (page 23)
Chinese Chicken Wings (page 21)
Sweet Walnuts (page 125)
Glögg (page 29)

Chinese Chicken Wings (page 21), Glögg (page 29),
Tangy Crab Meat Dip (page 27)

PIQUANT PINTO DIP

2 tablespoons butter or margarine
1 small onion, chopped
1 clove garlic, minced
1 can (15 ounces) pinto beans, drained
2 tablespoons chopped canned green chilies
1 tablespoon lime juice
Salt and freshly ground pepper to taste
½ cup (2 ounces) grated sharp Cheddar cheese
Nacho or tostada chips to serve

Melt butter in 2-quart saucepan over medium heat. Add onion and garlic and sauté until transparent.

Reduce heat to low. Add beans, chilies, lime juice, salt, and pepper. Cover and cook until hot and bubbly, stirring occasionally to prevent sticking.

Spoon dip into serving bowl and sprinkle cheese over top. Serve with chips.

about 1 cup

HONEYED CHICKEN TIDBITS

2 cups seasoned dry bread crumbs
½ cup (2 ounces) grated Parmesan cheese
2 tablespoons chopped fresh parsley
1 teaspoon poultry seasoning
½ teaspoon salt
1 egg
1½ pounds chicken cutlets, cut in 1-inch pieces
4 tablespoons vegetable oil, divided
Honey Lime Sauce (page 106)

Line 2 baking sheets with waxed paper. Combine bread crumbs, cheese, parsley, poultry seasoning, and salt in shallow dish. Place egg in small bowl and beat lightly.

Dip chicken pieces in egg and then in bread crumb mixture. Place on waxed paper. Repeat dipping procedure with egg and bread crumbs. Place breaded chicken on waxed paper-lined baking sheets. Cover and refrigerate 4 hours.

Heat 2 tablespoons oil in gourmet frying pan over medium heat. Add half the chicken pieces and fry until chicken is cooked and golden brown on all sides. Remove with slotted spoon and drain on paper towels. Add remaining 2 tablespoons oil to pan. Fry remaining chicken pieces and drain.

Serve hot with Honey Lime Sauce.

about 36 pieces

TANGY CRAB MEAT DIP

1 package (8 ounces) cream cheese, softened
1 tablespoon milk
1 package (6 ounces) frozen crab meat, thawed and drained
2 green onions, thinly sliced
½ teaspoon prepared horseradish
½ teaspoon Worcestershire sauce
Salt to taste
⅛ teaspoon lemon pepper
⅛ teaspoon hot pepper sauce
Paprika for garnish
Crudités and crackers to serve

Place cream cheese and milk in 1-quart saucepan and stir until smooth. Add crab meat, green onions, horseradish, Worcestershire, salt, lemon pepper, and hot pepper sauce. Stir until blended.

Simmer until just warm, stirring occasionally. Spoon into serving dish and garnish with paprika. Serve warm with crudités and crackers.

about 2 cups   *(See photo page 25)*

HOT ALPINE COCOA

¾ cup unsweetened cocoa powder
⅓ cup sugar
2 quarts milk
⅛ teaspoon salt
½ teaspoon vanilla
½ cup heavy cream, whipped, and nutmeg for garnish

Combine cocoa powder and sugar in Dutch oven. Gradually add milk and stir until blended. Stir in salt. Cover and simmer until heated through, stirring occasionally.

Remove from heat. Stir in vanilla. Ladle into mugs. Garnish each mug with dollop of whipped cream and sprinkle with nutmeg.

8 servings   *(See photo page 104)*

HOT CRANBERRY WINE

1 quart cranberry juice
2 cups apple juice
¼ cup lime juice
½ cup sugar
2 sticks cinnamon
6 whole cloves
2 cups sparkling red wine
12 lime slices

Combine cranberry juice, apple juice, lime juice, sugar, cinnamon, and cloves in Dutch oven. Simmer until sugar is dissolved.

Cover and continue to simmer 15 minutes. Stir in wine and simmer until heated through. Remove cinnamon sticks and cloves. Place lime slices in cups and pour in hot punch.

12 servings   *(See photo page 120)*

GLÖGG

3 cups Burgundy
3 cups dry sherry
1 cup brandy
½ cup sugar
1 cup dark seedless raisins
Peel of 2 oranges, cut in thin strips
Peel of 1 lemon, cut in thin strips
8 whole cloves
16 to 18 cinnamon sticks
½ teaspoon ground cardamom
Lemon slices for garnish

Combine Burgundy, sherry, brandy, and sugar in Dutch oven. Stir until blended. Cover and cook over medium heat until hot but not boiling.

Reduce heat to low. Add raisins, orange peel, lemon peel, cloves, 2 cinnamon sticks, and cardamom. Stir well. Cover and simmer 20 to 30 minutes to allow flavors to blend. Serve warm in mugs, garnished with lemon slices, with remaining cinnamon sticks inserted as stirrers.

14 to 16 servings   *(See photo page 25)*

Classic Ratatouille (page 99), Creamy French Onion Soup
(page 33), Chived Chicken Buns (page 44)

Chapter Two
Lighter Fare

WHITE BEAN SOUP

1 can (16 ounces) whole tomatoes, broken up
1 can (15 ounces) Great Northern beans, undrained
1 can (8 ounces) tomato sauce
1 cup cubed cooked ham
2 stalks celery, chopped
1 medium-size onion, chopped
2 cloves garlic, minced
2 cups beef broth
Salt and freshly ground pepper to taste

Combine tomatoes, beans, tomato sauce, ham, celery, onion, and garlic in Dutch oven. Add beef broth, salt, and pepper, and stir. Cover and cook over medium-high heat until soup comes to a boil. Reduce heat to medium-low and simmer 20 to 30 minutes.

4 servings

FRENCH VEGETABLE SOUP

2 large leeks
2 tablespoons butter or margarine
4 green onions, chopped
2 stalks celery, thinly sliced
2 carrots, thinly sliced
1 medium-size zucchini, thinly sliced
1 medium-size turnip, cut in cubes
2 cups tomato juice
2 cups beef broth
½ teaspoon basil
1 teaspoon salt
½ teaspoon freshly ground pepper
½ cup dairy sour cream to serve
2 tablespoons chopped fresh parsley for garnish

Trim leeks, discarding green tops. Quarter lengthwise and wash under cold water, pulling layers apart to rinse thoroughly. Chop leeks.

Melt butter in Dutch oven over medium heat. Add leeks, green onions, celery, carrots, zucchini, and turnip, and sauté 10 minutes.

Add tomato juice, beef broth, basil, salt, and pepper. Reduce heat to low. Cover and simmer 20 to 30 minutes or until all vegetables are tender.

Ladle into serving bowls. Top with dollop of sour cream and parsley.

6 servings

CREAMY FRENCH ONION SOUP

¼ cup butter or margarine
4 large onions, sliced (about 4 cups)
2 teaspoons sugar
2 tablespoons chopped fresh chives
2 tablespoons all-purpose flour
½ teaspoon salt
¼ teaspoon freshly ground pepper
2 cups beef broth
1½ cups light cream or milk
½ cup dry sherry
1 cup (4 ounces) grated Swiss cheese
Chopped chives for garnish

Melt butter in Dutch oven over medium heat. Add onions and sugar and sauté until onions are transparent and golden brown. Sprinkle chives, flour, salt, and pepper over onions and stir until well mixed. Cook 1 minute.

Add beef broth and cream to pan slowly, stirring. Cover and cook until mixture comes to a boil. Reduce heat to low, cover, and simmer 20 to 30 minutes. Stir in sherry, cook 2 minutes, and ladle into serving bowls. Sprinkle cheese and chives over top of soup before serving.

4 servings   *(See photo page 30)*

Note: *To help the cheese melt quickly, spoon hot soup over cheese.*

VICHYSSOISE

1 tablespoon butter or margarine
3 leeks (white part only), thinly sliced
1 small onion, thinly sliced
½ cup diced celery
1½ cups chicken broth
3 medium-size potatoes, peeled and diced
1 cup milk
½ teaspoon salt
¼ teaspoon white pepper
1 cup light cream
Chopped chives for garnish

Bring ¼ cup water to a boil in 3-quart saucepan over medium-high heat. Add butter, leeks, onion, and celery, and cook 5 minutes or until onion is transparent. Add broth and potatoes. Reduce heat to medium and cook 15 minutes.

Add milk. Increase heat to medium-high. Bring just to a boil. Remove from heat and season with salt and white pepper.

Place soup, 2 cups at a time, in container of blender and process until puréed. Chill thoroughly. Stir in light cream and serve in chilled soup bowls. Garnish each serving with chopped chives.

4 servings   *(See photo page 43)*

CAULIFLOWER BISQUE

1 small head cauliflower
3 tablespoons butter or margarine
¼ cup chopped onion
¼ cup chopped celery
3 tablespoons all-purpose flour
3 cups chicken broth
1 cup light cream
1 cup (4 ounces) shredded Cheddar cheese, divided
⅛ teaspoon summer savory
Salt and freshly ground pepper to taste
Chopped fresh parsley for garnish

Trim leaves from cauliflower and break into flowerets. Cook in lightly salted water in 3-quart saucepan over medium-high heat about 10 minutes or until just tender. Drain and set aside in saucepan.

Meanwhile, melt butter in 2-quart saucepan. Add onion and celery and sauté until onion is transparent. Stir in flour and cook 1 minute. Add chicken broth and cream slowly, stirring constantly. Cook over low heat until slightly thickened. Add ½ cup cheese and cook, stirring, until cheese is melted.

Pour soup over well-drained cauliflower and stir. Season with summer savory, salt, and pepper. Reduce heat to low and cook until just heated through. Ladle into bowls and top with remaining ½ cup cheese. Garnish with chopped parsley.

4 servings

CRAB MEAT BISQUE FLORENTINE

2 tablespoons butter or margarine
2 tablespoons all-purpose flour
2 cups light cream or milk
½ cup chicken broth
1 package (10 ounces) frozen chopped spinach,
thawed and drained
1 package (8 ounces) frozen crab meat,
thawed and drained
2 green onions, chopped
1 tablespoon chopped fresh parsley
1 teaspoon Worcestershire sauce
½ teaspoon salt
⅛ teaspoon white pepper
⅛ teaspoon hot pepper sauce

Melt butter in 3-quart saucepan over medium heat. Add flour and cook 1 minute. Gradually add cream and chicken broth, stirring constantly. Cook until slightly thickened.

Add spinach, crab meat, green onions, parsley, Worcestershire, salt, white pepper, and hot pepper sauce. Reduce heat to low, cover, and simmer 20 minutes.

4 servings

NEW ENGLAND CLAM CHOWDER

4 slices bacon, diced
1 tablespoon butter or margarine
1 medium-size onion, chopped
1½ cups light cream
1½ cups milk, divided
2 cans (6½ ounces each) clams, drained, liquid reserved
2 large potatoes, peeled and diced
1 teaspoon thyme
1 teaspoon salt
¼ teaspoon freshly ground pepper
2 tablespoons cornstarch

Fry bacon in Dutch oven over medium heat until crisp. Remove bacon with slotted spoon and drain on paper towel. Discard bacon fat. Melt butter in Dutch oven, add onion, and sauté until transparent. Gradually stir light cream, 1 cup milk, reserved clam liquid, potatoes, thyme, salt, and pepper into onion.

Reduce heat to low. Cover and cook 15 to 20 minutes or until potatoes are tender. Combine remaining ½ cup milk and cornstarch in small bowl. Stir until smooth. Add cornstarch mixture and clams to chowder, stirring until blended. Cover and cook 5 to 10 minutes or until slightly thickened.

4 servings

GARDEN POTATO SALAD

1 medium-size zucchini, sliced
1 cup shredded carrots
½ cup fresh green peas
6 medium-size red boiling potatoes, cooked, peeled,
and sliced
2 green onions, chopped
¾ cup mayonnaise
½ to ¾ cup dairy sour cream
1 teaspoon prepared mustard
1 teaspoon dillweed
1 teaspoon salt
½ teaspoon freshly ground pepper

Combine zucchini, carrots, and peas in 3-quart saucepan. Add ¼ cup hot water. Cover and cook over medium heat until just tender. Drain and cool.

Mix potatoes, zucchini mixture, and green onions in large bowl. Combine mayonnaise, sour cream, mustard, dillweed, salt, and pepper in small bowl. Add to vegetables and stir gently to coat. Spoon into serving bowl.

Cover and chill several hours to allow flavors to blend.

6 to 8 servings

Note: *To cook potatoes, place in Dutch oven, and add water to cover. Cook over medium-high heat until potatoes are tender. Drain, peel, and cool.*

GERMAN POTATO SALAD

4 slices bacon, diced
1 medium-size onion, chopped
1 stalk celery, thinly sliced
2 tablespoons sugar
1 tablespoon all-purpose flour
2 tablespoons cider vinegar
2 tablespoons lemon juice
1 teaspoon salt
¼ teaspoon freshly ground pepper
4 medium-size potatoes, cooked, peeled, and sliced
(about 4 cups)
1 tablespoon minced fresh parsley for garnish

Fry bacon in gourmet frying pan over medium-high heat until crisp. Remove bacon with slotted spoon and drain on paper towel. Pour off all but 2 tablespoons drippings from frying pan. Add onion and celery and sauté until tender.

Combine sugar and flour in small bowl. Add vinegar, lemon juice, 1 cup water, salt, and pepper. Stir until blended. Stir into onion mixture and cook over medium heat, stirring constantly, until thickened.

Combine bacon and potatoes in large bowl. Pour hot dressing over potatoes and toss gently to coat. Sprinkle with parsley. Serve warm.

4 servings

TEX-MEX SALAD

FIRST LAYER
1 package (8 ounces) cream cheese, softened
1 envelope (1⅝ ounces) chili seasoning mix
½ teaspoon lemon juice
Dash hot pepper sauce

SECOND LAYER
1 pound lean ground beef
1 small onion, chopped
1 small green pepper, chopped
2 or 3 canned jalapeño peppers, seeded and chopped
1 teaspoon chili powder
1 small head lettuce

THIRD LAYER
2 medium-size tomatoes, seeded and coarsely chopped
¼ cup sliced ripe olives
2 green onions, sliced
½ cup (2 ounces) grated Cheddar cheese

Mild or hot taco sauce to serve
Nacho or tostada chips to serve

To prepare first layer, place cream cheese and chili seasoning mix in small mixing bowl. Beat with electric mixer at medium speed until smooth. Add lemon juice and hot pepper sauce and beat until well combined. Spread evenly over bottom of 14-inch round serving platter, covering surface completely. Set aside.

To prepare second layer, cook beef in gourmet frying pan over medium heat until browned. Drain off excess fat. Add onion, green pepper, jalapeño peppers, and chili powder. Sauté until vegetables are tender. Set aside and cool to room temperature. Tear lettuce into bite-size pieces and arrange over first layer. Spoon beef mixture over lettuce.

To prepare third layer, arrange tomatoes, olives, green onions, and cheese over beef.

Serve with taco sauce and chips.

4 to 6 servings

GRILLED ROAST BEEF SANDWICHES

Butter or margarine
8 slices French bread
1 pound thinly sliced roast beef
1 medium-size red onion, sliced
4 thick slices mozzarella cheese (about 4 ounces)
½ teaspoon Italian seasoning
½ teaspoon salt
¼ teaspoon freshly ground pepper
Crushed red pepper to taste (optional)
Prepared mustard to taste (optional)

Butter both sides of bread slices. Divide beef evenly on 4 slices. Place onion and cheese slices on top of beef. Sprinkle Italian seasoning, salt, pepper, and red pepper, if desired, over each sandwich.

Spread mustard, if desired, on remaining 4 bread slices. Place slices on prepared sandwiches. Preheat gourmet frying pan over medium heat. Add sandwiches, 1 at a time, and grill, turning once, until bread is golden brown and cheese melts. (If sandwiches are browning too quickly, reduce heat to medium-low.)

4 servings

AMERICAN BURGERS

1 pound lean ground beef
1 small onion, chopped
1 tablespoon barbecue sauce
Salt and freshly ground pepper to taste
4 hamburger buns, split and warmed

Combine beef, onion, barbecue sauce, salt, and pepper in medium-size bowl. Stir until well mixed. Shape mixture into 4 patties, each about 1 inch thick.

Fry patties in gourmet frying pan over medium heat 3 to 4 minutes on each side or to desired doneness.

Place patties in hamburger buns.

4 servings

BEEF-AND-SAUSAGE PATTIES

½ pound lean ground beef
½ pound Italian sausage
1 small onion, chopped
1 clove garlic, minced
1 teaspoon prepared mustard
½ teaspoon salt
¼ teaspoon freshly ground pepper
4 crusty hard rolls

Combine beef, sausage, onion, garlic, mustard, salt, and pepper in medium-size bowl. Stir until well mixed. Shape mixture into 4 patties, each about 1 inch thick.

Fry patties in gourmet frying pan over medium heat 4 to 5 minutes on each side or to desired doneness.

Place patties in rolls.

4 servings

BARBECUED PORK SANDWICHES

2 tablespoons vegetable oil
1 pound boneless pork, cut in thin strips
1 medium-size onion, sliced
¾ cup barbecue sauce
2 tablespoons molasses
1 teaspoon Worcestershire sauce
4 crusty hard rolls

Heat oil in 3-quart saucepan over medium heat. Add pork and brown quickly. Add onion, barbecue sauce, molasses, and Worcestershire, and stir. Cover and cook, stirring occasionally, until hot and bubbly.

Spoon onto rolls.

4 servings

Menu:
Light Lunch for Four

Vichyssoise (page 34)
Turkey-Jack Croissants (page 45)
chilled dry white wine
sorbet and assorted butter cookies

Vichyssoise (page 34), Turkey-Jack Croissants (page 45)

GOLDEN TUNA SALAD SANDWICHES

1 can (3½ ounces) tuna, drained
1 green onion, chopped
2 tablespoons finely chopped celery
¼ teaspoon prepared mustard
¼ teaspoon dillweed
⅓ cup grated Swiss cheese
¼ to ⅓ cup mayonnaise
8 slices whole-wheat bread
8 slices tomato
4 tablespoons butter or margarine, divided

Combine tuna, green onion, celery, mustard, and dillweed. Stir until well mixed. Add cheese and mayonnaise and stir until moistened.

Divide filling into 4 portions and spread on bread slices. Arrange 2 slices tomato on each sandwich. Top with remaining bread slices.

Melt 1 tablespoon butter in gourmet frying pan over medium heat. Add 1 sandwich and cook until golden brown on both sides. Repeat with remaining butter and sandwiches.

4 servings

CHIVED CHICKEN BUNS

2 chicken cutlets, ground (about ¾ pound)
1 cup fresh bread crumbs, divided
4 tablespoons butter or margarine, divided
¼ cup milk
1 tablespoon chopped fresh chives
½ teaspoon Italian seasoning
Salt to taste
¼ teaspoon lemon pepper
Dijon-style mustard (optional)
4 rye or kaiser rolls, warmed
Curly leaf lettuce and fresh chives for garnish

Combine chicken, ½ cup bread crumbs, 1 tablespoon butter, milk, chives, Italian seasoning, salt, and lemon pepper in bowl.

Mix well. Shape mixture into 4 patties, each about ½ inch thick. Place remaining ½ cup bread crumbs in small dish. Press patties into crumbs, coating patties completely.

Melt remaining 3 tablespoons butter in gourmet frying pan. Fry patties 4 to 5 minutes on each side or until browned and crisp.

Spread mustard on bottom half of rolls, if desired, top with lettuce, and place patties over lettuce. Top with additional mustard, garnish with chives, and cover with top half of rolls.

4 servings   *(See photo page 30)*

TURKEY-JACK CROISSANTS

1 tablespoon butter or margarine
3 green onions, sliced
1 stalk celery, chopped
3 cups cubed cooked turkey
1 envelope (⅞ ounce) chicken gravy mix
½ teaspoon dillweed
½ cup dairy sour cream
2 tablespoons sweet relish, drained
4 to 6 croissants, split and warmed
4 to 6 thick slices Monterey Jack or brick cheese
(about 4 to 6 ounces)
4 to 6 cherry tomatoes, parsley sprigs, and green onion strips for garnish (optional)

Melt butter in 2-quart saucepan over medium heat. Add green onions and celery and sauté until tender. Add turkey and cook until heated through, stirring occasionally.

Reduce heat to low. Sprinkle gravy mix and dillweed over turkey and stir to coat. Remove from heat. Add sour cream and relish and stir until well mixed.

Spoon onto croissants. Top with cheese slice. If desired, garnish with cherry tomato stuffed with parsley, and green onion.

4 to 6 servings   *(See photo page 43)*

CHILE PICANTE

1 pound lean ground beef
1 medium-size onion, diced
1 tablespoon chopped canned green chilies (optional)
1 to 2 teaspoons chili powder
½ teaspoon ground cumin
1 clove garlic, minced
1 can (16 ounces) stewed tomatoes
1 can (15 ounces) red kidney beans, undrained
1 can (6 ounces) tomato paste
½ cup beef broth
Salt and freshly ground pepper to taste
Cayenne to taste

Brown beef and onion in 3-quart saucepan over medium heat. Drain off excess fat. Add chilies, if desired, chili powder, cumin, and garlic. Stir until well mixed. Cover and cook 5 minutes. Stir tomatoes, kidney beans, tomato paste, beef broth, salt, pepper, and cayenne into beef mixture. Cover and cook 20 to 30 minutes to allow flavors to blend.

4 to 6 servings

DEEP-PAN PIZZA

1 package (6½ ounces) pizza crust mix
½ pound lean ground beef
1 small onion, chopped
¼ cup chopped green pepper
1 can (8 ounces) tomato sauce
½ teaspoon fennel
1 teaspoon Italian seasoning
1 cup (4 ounces) shredded mozzarella cheese
2 tablespoons grated Parmesan cheese

Preheat oven to 400°F. Prepare pizza crust mix according to package directions. Pat into gourmet frying pan. Bake 10 minutes.

Meanwhile, brown beef in 2-quart saucepan over medium heat. Add onion and green pepper and sauté until onion is transparent. Drain off excess fat. Set aside.

Pour tomato sauce evenly over hot crust. Sprinkle fennel and Italian seasoning over sauce. Spoon beef mixture evenly over top. Sprinkle mozzarella cheese over beef. Bake 20 minutes or until cheese melts and sauce is set. Sprinkle Parmesan cheese over hot pizza and cut into serving-size wedges.

2 servings

SPINACH PAN SOUFFLÉ

1 package (10 ounces) frozen chopped spinach,
thawed and drained
1 container (8 ounces) prepared dairy sour
cream and onion dip, divided
½ cup seasoned dry bread crumbs
1 egg
1 teaspoon lemon juice
Salt and freshly ground pepper to taste
2 tablespoons butter or margarine
2 large tomatoes, cut in ½-inch slices
¼ cup grated Parmesan cheese
½ teaspoon dillweed

Combine spinach, half the sour cream dip, bread crumbs, egg, lemon juice, salt, and pepper in small bowl. Stir until well mixed.

Melt butter in gourmet frying pan over medium heat. Spoon spinach mixture into frying pan. Layer tomato slices over spinach. Place dollop of remaining sour cream dip on each tomato slice and sprinkle cheese over top.

Cover and cook 5 minutes. Reduce heat to medium-low and continue to cook 5 minutes or until spinach is set. Sprinkle dillweed on top and serve directly from skillet.

4 servings

POACHED EGG

1 teaspoon vinegar
½ teaspoon salt
1 egg
1 slice buttered toast

Place 1 cup water, vinegar, and salt in 1-quart saucepan and bring to a slow boil over medium-high heat.

Break egg into small bowl. Ease egg into water. Reduce heat to low and simmer 1 or 2 minutes or until white is set. Remove with slotted spoon and drain well. Place on toast.

1 serving

Helpful hint: *For perfectly shaped poached eggs, bring water to a boil in small saucepan. Swirl boiling water with spoon and ease egg into well formed in center.*

POACHED EGGS FLORENTINE

1 tablespoon butter or margarine
1 small onion, chopped
1 package (10 ounces) frozen chopped spinach,
thawed and drained
¼ teaspoon grated lemon peel
⅛ teaspoon nutmeg
Salt and freshly ground pepper to taste
White Sauce (page 102)
¼ cup (1 ounce) grated Swiss cheese
½ teaspoon Dijon-style mustard
4 slices tomato
4 Poached Eggs (above)
Paprika for garnish

Melt butter in gourmet frying pan over medium heat. Add onion and sauté until transparent. Add spinach, lemon peel, nutmeg, salt, and pepper, and cook until spinach is heated through. Cover and set aside.

Place White Sauce in 1-quart saucepan. Stir in cheese and mustard and cook over low heat until cheese melts. Set aside. Divide hot spinach evenly on 4 individual serving dishes. Arrange tomato slice and Poached Egg on each dish of spinach. Quickly reheat sauce, if necessary, and spoon sauce over Poached Eggs.

Garnish with paprika.

4 servings

WELSH RABBIT

4 slices bacon
1 tablespoon butter or margarine
½ teaspoon dry mustard
¾ cup beer
1 teaspoon Worcestershire sauce
Cayenne to taste
2 cups (8 ounces) coarsely grated sharp Cheddar cheese
2 English muffins, split and toasted
4 slices tomato

Fry bacon in gourmet frying pan over medium heat until crisp. Remove with slotted spoon and drain on paper towel.

Melt butter in 2-quart saucepan over medium heat. Stir in mustard until smooth. Add beer, Worcestershire, and cayenne. Stir well, reduce heat, and simmer 4 to 5 minutes. Add cheese gradually, stirring constantly. Cook until cheese melts.

Spoon cheese mixture over English muffins. Top each muffin half with tomato and bacon slice.

4 servings

FLUFFY EGG SCRAMBLE

3 tablespoons butter or margarine
6 eggs
½ cup milk
Salt and freshly ground pepper to taste

Melt butter in gourmet frying pan over medium heat. Remove from heat. Combine eggs and milk in large bowl. Spoon 2 tablespoons melted butter into egg mixture. Add salt and pepper and beat until frothy.

Pour egg mixture into pan and cook over medium heat until set, stirring constantly to let uncooked portion flow to bottom of pan.

3 to 4 servings

SCRAMBLED EGGS
CALIFORNIA-STYLE

8 eggs
¼ cup milk
Salt and freshly ground pepper to taste
2 tablespoons butter or margarine
1 package (6 ounces) frozen small shrimp,
thawed and drained
1 small avocado, peeled, pitted, and coarsely chopped
½ cup (2 ounces) shredded Monterey Jack cheese
1 tablespoon chopped fresh chives

Beat eggs, milk, salt, and pepper with fork in medium-size bowl. Set aside.

Melt butter in gourmet frying pan over medium heat. Swirl to coat bottom of pan. Pour in egg mixture and cook until almost set, stirring lightly to let uncooked portion flow to bottom of pan.

Arrange shrimp and avocado over eggs and stir lightly. Sprinkle cheese and chives over egg mixture and cook just until eggs are set.

4 servings

SCRAMBLED EGGS MANHATTAN-STYLE

8 eggs
¼ cup milk
1 teaspoon Dijon-style mustard
Freshly ground pepper to taste
2 tablespoons butter or margarine
1 small onion, chopped
2 ounces thinly sliced smoked salmon, chopped

Beat eggs, milk, mustard, and pepper with fork in medium-size bowl. Set aside.

Melt butter in gourmet frying pan over medium heat. Add onion and sauté until transparent. Swirl to coat bottom of pan. Pour in egg mixture and cook until almost set, stirring lightly to let uncooked portion flow to bottom of pan.

Add salmon and stir lightly. Cook just until eggs are set.

4 servings

SCRAMBLED EGGS FARM-STYLE

8 eggs
¼ cup milk
Salt and freshly ground pepper to taste
2 tablespoons butter or margarine
2 ounces thinly sliced corned beef, cut in strips
½ cup cooked peas
½ cup (2 ounces) shredded Cheddar or brick cheese
1 cup White Sauce (page 102), warmed, to serve

Beat eggs, milk, salt, and pepper with fork in medium-size bowl. Set aside.

Melt butter in gourmet frying pan over medium heat. Swirl to coat bottom of pan. Pour in egg mixture and cook until almost set, stirring lightly to let uncooked portion flow to bottom of pan.

Add beef and peas and stir lightly. Sprinkle cheese over egg mixture and cook just until eggs are set. Spoon onto warm serving platter. Serve with White Sauce.

4 servings

CHEESE AND MUSHROOM OMELET

2 tablespoons butter or margarine
2 eggs
1 tablespoon milk
Salt and freshly ground pepper to taste
4 tablespoons (1 ounce) shredded Cheddar or
brick cheese, divided
¼ cup Creamy Mushroom Sauce (page 102), warmed

Preheat gourmet frying pan. Melt butter over medium heat. Remove from heat. Combine eggs and milk in small bowl. Add salt and pepper. Spoon 1 tablespoon melted butter into egg mixture. Beat until light and fluffy.

Rotate pan over medium heat to spread remaining melted butter. When pan is hot, pour in egg mixture. Cook until edges are set, gently lifting edges with spatula to let uncooked portion flow to bottom of pan.

Sprinkle 2 tablespoons cheese evenly over top of omelet and fold in half. Place on serving plate and spoon mushroom sauce over omelet. Sprinkle remaining 2 tablespoons cheese on top.

1 serving

MAPLE FRENCH TOAST

2 eggs
2 tablespoons milk
1 tablespoon maple syrup
¼ teaspoon nutmeg
4 thick slices French bread
4 teaspoons butter or margarine
Maple syrup, warmed, to serve

Combine eggs, milk, syrup, and nutmeg in shallow dish. Dip bread slices, 1 at a time, in egg mixture. Coat bread well and allow bread slices to absorb all the egg mixture.

Preheat gourmet frying pan. Melt 2 teaspoons butter over medium heat. Add 2 bread slices and cook until golden brown on both sides. Repeat with remaining butter and bread.

Serve hot with warm maple syrup.

2 servings

BLUEBERRY BUTTERMILK PANCAKES

1¼ cups all-purpose flour
¼ cup sugar
2 teaspoons baking soda
½ teaspoon salt
½ teaspoon grated lemon peel
1 egg
1 cup buttermilk
½ cup frozen blueberries, drained
8 teaspoons vegetable oil
Butter or margarine to serve
Honey or maple syrup, warmed, to serve

Combine flour, sugar, baking soda, salt, and lemon peel in large bowl. Set aside.

Beat egg and buttermilk in small bowl. Stir into flour mixture until just moistened. Fold in blueberries.

Preheat gourmet frying pan over medium heat until drop of water sizzles. Add 1 teaspoon oil and swirl to coat bottom of pan. Reduce heat to medium-low. Pour ¼ cup batter into frying pan and cook until pancake is bubbly and edges begin to dry. Turn pancake over and cook until bottom is golden brown. Repeat with remaining oil and batter. Serve hot with butter and honey or maple syrup.

about 8 pancakes

(See photo page 104)

Note: *Substitute fresh blueberries for frozen when available. For thinner pancakes, use 1¼ cups buttermilk. For a decorative touch, reserve a few blueberries for garnish.*

Recipes from the Better LifePlans Institute

Most of us know we should be eating better ... exercising more ... reducing stress and the stress-related practices in our lives. But somehow we never seem able to convert that knowledge into action, to make new and better health habits a permanent, integral, comfortable part of our daily routine.

At the Better LifePlans Institute, individuals and families learn how to take that great leap *beyond* good intentions. Through the Institute's intensive, highly structured seven- and ten-day programs, participants not only improve their knowledge of the best-available scientific and medical health information but actually learn to practice the behavior-change and psychological skills that are essential for establishing and maintaining good health on a lifelong basis.

The Institute's programs are targeted to these six critical goals:

1. weight reduction and control

2. reduction and control of high blood pressure, high cholesterol, high blood sugar, and cigarette smoking

3. improved exercise and physical fitness

4. improved stress management techniques

5. reduction of certain cancer risks associated with nutritional factors

6. prevention of disease and maintenance of health through improved nutrition, exercise, and reduced stress-related practices.

In concentrated seven- and ten-day residential programs, Institute participants learn that better health is a reward for "players," not "spectators." Through staff-directed discussion sessions, individually tailored exercise classes, healthful, calorie-controlled snacks and meals, and cooking laboratories as well as other "real-world" behavior training situations, individuals learn to take charge of reassessing and restructuring their basic health behavior patterns. As graduates of the program, they take home a new, healthful "blueprint for living." At the heart of that LifePlan blueprint: a maintenance system of motivational and behavioral materials, foods, nutritional supplements, and fitness equipment designed to support healthy and enjoyable living habits for a lifetime.

Good nutritional and weight control habits, Institute graduates have learned, are not a matter of discovering a new "fad" health regimen or diet. Instead, we must learn to take the nutritional factors that scientific consensus tells us are the building blocks of sound health and incorporate them in our daily lives. The Better LifePlans Institute helps participants sort their way through the many health recommendations and controversies prevalent today by teaching them to recognize the distinctions between advocacy, faddism, scientific fact, and informed judgment. Both the seven-day program at the four-star Amway Grand Plaza Hotel in Grand Rapids, Michigan, and the ten-day Peter Island program, at Amway's idyllic private island in the Caribbean, provide ideal learning-oriented environments set in luxurious, world-class accommodations.

On the following pages are some of the favorite recipes of staff and participants at both Better LifePlans Institute locations. Like all Institute creations, these recipes apply one simple, overriding principle: in order to be effective, any nutrition or behavior-change plan must be both scientifically sound and easily practiced and enjoyed. The healthful foods used in these recipes — vegetables, fruit, whole grains, chicken, fish — give us dishes that are naturally high in fiber and low in calories, sugar, salt, additives, fat, and cholesterol. But most importantly, these dishes are simple to prepare, look attractive and tempting on the plate, and taste absolutely delicious. They are a delightful demonstration of the fact that, with the proper knowledge and basic behavioral and psychological tools, anyone can make healthful foods the center of an enjoyable, life-enriching diet . . . and of a healthy, successful LifePlan.

VEGETABLE CHEESE BALLS

Never Stik
½ cup sliced mushrooms
½ cup sliced onion
½ cup sliced carrots
½ cup minced fresh parsley
1 clove garlic, minced
1 package (8 ounces) low-calorie process cheese slices
1 teaspoon dry mustard
Seasoned Bread Crumbs (page 62) or
crunchy nutlike cereal nuggets
Cocktail sauce to serve

Spray gourmet frying pan with Never Stik, and sauté mushrooms, onion, carrots, parsley, and garlic until crisp-tender. Remove from heat and set aside to cool. Place vegetables, cheese, and mustard in container of food processor and process until smooth. (Mixture will be very thick.) Spoon into bowl, cover, and refrigerate until firm. Moisten hands with water and form mixture into walnut-size balls. Roll balls in bread crumbs and refrigerate until firm. Serve with cocktail sauce.

24 appetizers

ASPARAGUS BISQUE

2 packages (10 ounces each) frozen asparagus spears
3 cups defatted chicken stock
1 medium-size onion, chopped
1 tablespoon lemon juice
1 teaspoon curry powder
Water or milk

Place asparagus, stock, onion, lemon juice, and curry powder in Dutch oven. Cover and bring to a boil over medium-high heat. Reduce heat and simmer until asparagus is tender. Transfer in batches to container of blender or food processor and process until smooth. Return to Dutch oven. Add water or milk to desired consistency. Simmer until heated through.

6 to 8 servings

STUFFED MUSHROOMS

Never Stik
1 slice toasted French or sourdough bread
12 large mushrooms
1 small onion, chopped
1 clove garlic, minced
1 tablespoon minced fresh parsley
½ teaspoon Italian seasoning
⅛ teaspoon freshly ground pepper
2 tablespoons defatted chicken stock

Spray baking sheet with Never Stik. Place toast in container of
blender or food processor and process until crumbed. Set aside.
Clean mushrooms with damp cloth and remove stems. Set caps
aside and chop stems. Spray gourmet frying pan with Never Stik,
and sauté mushroom stems, onion, garlic, and parsley until onion
is transparent. Add reserved bread crumbs, Italian seasoning,
pepper, and chicken stock. Mix well and spoon into mushroom
caps. Place caps on prepared baking sheet, stuffed-side up, and
broil 3 to 4 minutes or until browned on top.

12 appetizers

HOT AND SOUR SOUP

4 cups defatted vegetable, chicken, or beef stock
2 tablespoons sodium-reduced soy sauce
¼ teaspoon crushed red pepper
1 cup shredded Chinese cabbage
½ cup frozen or fresh corn kernels
½ cup chopped celery
½ pound tofu, diced
2 tablespoons lemon juice
2 tablespoons cornstarch

Place stock, soy sauce, and red pepper in 3-quart saucepan.
Bring to a boil over medium-high heat. Stir in cabbage, corn, and
celery. Reduce heat and simmer about 10 minutes. Add tofu and
lemon juice. Simmer 10 minutes. Combine cornstarch and ¼ cup
water in small bowl. Stir until smooth. Add to soup and simmer,
stirring, until thickened. Serve hot.

6 servings

POTATO PANCAKES

2 large potatoes, grated
1 small onion, grated
¼ cup all-purpose flour
1 teaspoon baking powder
¼ teaspoon onion powder
¼ teaspoon garlic powder
¼ teaspoon freshly ground pepper
3 egg whites
Never Stik
Applesauce (page 67) and
Whipped Cottage Cheese (below) to serve

Combine potatoes and onion in large bowl. Sprinkle flour, baking powder, onion powder, garlic powder, and pepper over potato-onion mixture and stir. Beat egg whites until stiff peaks form and fold into potato-onion mixture. Spray gourmet frying pan with Never Stik and preheat pan over low heat. Spoon batter into pan by rounded tablespoonfuls, spreading pancakes to ½-inch thickness. Cook slowly until pancakes are brown and crispy on bottom. Turn over and brown other side. Spray with additional Never Stik if needed and repeat with remaining batter. Serve pancakes hot with Applesauce and Whipped Cottage Cheese.

6 to 8 pancakes

WHIPPED COTTAGE CHEESE

1 container (1 pint) low-calorie cottage cheese

Place cottage cheese in container of blender or food processor and process until smooth. Chill, and serve as you would sour cream.

2 cups

STUFFED CHICKEN CUTLETS IN WINE-MUSHROOM SAUCE

4 chicken cutlets (about 1 pound)
4 tablespoons Poultry Stuffing (below)
Never Stik
About ¾ cup defatted chicken stock
About ¾ cup dry white wine
1 cup sliced mushrooms (about ½ pound)

Preheat oven to 350°F. Lightly pound chicken cutlets until flattened. Place 1 tablespoon stuffing on each cutlet. Roll up cutlets and secure with wooden toothpicks. Spray gourmet frying pan with Never Stik, and sauté chicken until browned on all sides. Combine chicken stock and wine, and pour enough into pan to cover bottom half of chicken. Add mushrooms. Bake 45 minutes or until chicken is cooked through, basting frequently.

4 servings

POULTRY STUFFING

Never Stik
1 cup chopped onion
1 cup chopped celery
¼ cup chopped fresh parsley
3 cloves garlic, minced
8 slices French, Italian, or sourdough bread,
torn in chunks
1 cup defatted chicken stock
1 cup evaporated skim milk
1 tablespoon poultry seasoning

Spray 2-quart saucepan with Never Stik, and sauté onion, celery, parsley, and garlic until onion is transparent. Add bread and stir to combine. Stir in chicken stock, milk, and poultry seasoning. Mix well.

6 to 8 cups

Note: *Add extra skim milk if a moister stuffing is desired.*

BOUILLABAISSE "THE EASY WAY"

3 bottles (8 ounces each) clam juice
¼ cup finely chopped onion
¼ cup finely chopped celery
Never Stik
2 leeks (white part only), thinly
sliced, or 1 large onion, chopped
1 clove garlic, minced
1 cup dry white wine
1 can (16 ounces) whole peeled tomatoes, undrained,
broken up
¾ teaspoon herbes de Provence
Pinch saffron threads
4 clams in shell, scrubbed, or 1 can (6 ½ ounces)
chopped or minced clams, drained
1 fish fillet (¼ pound), cut in chunks
¼ pound scallops
¼ pound medium-size shrimp, shelled and deveined
Crusty French bread to serve

Combine clam juice, 3 cups water, onion, and celery in Dutch oven. Bring to a boil, reduce heat, cover, and simmer 5 minutes. Spray gourmet frying pan with Never Stik, and sauté leeks and garlic until lightly browned. Add to clam juice mixture. Stir in wine, tomatoes and liquid, herbes de Provence, and saffron. Cover and simmer 5 minutes. Add clams, fish fillet, scallops, and shrimp. Cover and simmer 5 minutes or until all fish is tender. Adjust seasoning. Serve hot in large bowls with French bread.

6 servings

MEATBALLS

1 pound beef flank steak, trimmed and ground
1 cup Seasoned Bread Crumbs (page 62)
½ small onion, grated
1 tablespoon chopped fresh parsley
¼ teaspoon freshly ground pepper
1 clove garlic, minced
2 egg whites
Never Stik

Combine ground steak, bread crumbs, onion, parsley, pepper, garlic, and egg whites in large bowl. Form into walnut-size balls. Spray gourmet frying pan with Never Stik, and sauté meatballs until well browned on all sides. Serve with your choice of sauce.

4 to 6 servings

PASTA PRIMAVERA

1 package (12 ounces) spaghetti or other pasta
Never Stik
1 package (10 ounces) frozen Italian-style
vegetables, thawed
About 2 cups tomato or spaghetti sauce, divided
1 teaspoon Italian seasoning
Grated Parmesan cheese to taste
Chopped fresh parsley for garnish

Cook spaghetti in Dutch oven according to package directions until al dente. Drain well, spray Dutch oven with Never Stik, and return spaghetti to Dutch oven. Add vegetables, 1 cup sauce, and Italian seasoning. Toss gently. Place over low heat. Add additional sauce as needed and cheese, tossing gently to combine. Simmer just until vegetables are heated through. Garnish with parsley and serve hot with additional warmed sauce and cheese.

4 to 6 servings

Note: *For fuller flavor, add sautéed chopped onion and garlic to pasta mixture or sauce before serving. Sautéed chopped mushrooms, green pepper, and other vegetables can also be added for variety.*

SEASONED BREAD CRUMBS

6 slices toasted French, Italian, or sourdough bread,
cut in chunks
2 tablespoons grated Parmesan cheese
1 tablespoon parsley flakes
1 teaspoon Italian seasoning
½ teaspoon freshly ground pepper

Place toast, cheese, parsley, Italian seasoning, and pepper in container of blender or food processor. Process until mixture is consistency of crumbs. Store in covered container.

about 2 cups

RATATOUILLE

Never Stik
1 large onion, chopped
½ medium-size green pepper, chopped
2 cloves garlic, minced
2 medium-size zucchini, thinly sliced
1 small eggplant, peeled and cubed
1 can (28 ounces) crushed peeled tomatoes
¼ cup dry white wine
¼ cup chopped fresh parsley
1½ teaspoons Italian seasoning
Freshly ground pepper to taste

Spray gourmet frying pan with Never Stik, and sauté onion, green pepper, and garlic until lightly browned. Add zucchini, eggplant, tomatoes, wine, parsley, Italian seasoning, and pepper. Stir to combine. Reduce heat, cover, and simmer until vegetables are crisp-tender, stirring occasionally.

4 to 6 servings

ORIENTAL VEGETABLE SAUTÉ

Never Stik
2 stalks celery, cut in diagonal slices
1 large onion, coarsely chopped
1 large green pepper, cut in strips
1 large sweet red pepper, cut in strips
3 cloves garlic, minced
1 cup sliced mushrooms
1 cup drained canned bean sprouts
½ cup snow peas
½ cup drained sliced water chestnuts
1 tablespoon cornstarch
1 teaspoon Chinese spice seasoning
Freshly ground pepper to taste
1 cup defatted chicken stock
Soy sauce to taste
Hot cooked rice to serve (optional)

Spray gourmet frying pan with Never Stik, and sauté celery, onion, peppers, and garlic until crisp-tender. Reduce heat to low and add mushrooms, bean sprouts, snow peas, and water chestnuts. Stir to combine and cook 5 minutes. Place cornstarch, Chinese spice seasoning, and pepper in medium-size bowl. Add chicken stock and soy sauce gradually and stir until smooth. Stir into vegetable mixture. Simmer until sauce is thickened and clear and vegetables are heated through. Serve as side dish or over rice as meatless main dish.

4 to 6 servings

Note: *For extra low-calorie, cholesterol-free protein, add tofu cubes with chicken stock. Cooked chicken chunks, shrimp, scallops, or lobster may also be added to the vegetables to turn this side dish into a hearty main meal.*

SWEET AND SOUR CABBAGE

1 small red cabbage (about 1 pound), shredded
1 onion, finely chopped
1 apple, peeled and diced
1 cup Applesauce (page 67)
⅓ cup vinegar
¼ cup undiluted apple juice concentrate
¼ teaspoon ground cloves

Combine cabbage, onion, apple, Applesauce, vinegar, apple juice concentrate, and cloves in Dutch oven. Cover and cook over low heat until crisp-tender, adding additional liquid during cooking if needed.

6 to 8 servings

Note: *For fuller flavor, add ¼ to ½ cup defatted beef stock.*

LEMON RICE

Never Stik
½ onion, finely chopped
1 clove garlic, finely minced
1 cup brown rice
2½ cups defatted chicken stock
¼ cup finely chopped fresh parsley
Grated peel of 1 lemon
1 teaspoon lemon juice

Spray 2-quart saucepan with Never Stik, and sauté onion and garlic until onion is transparent. Stir in rice, 1 cup water, and chicken stock. Cover, bring to a boil, reduce heat, and simmer 45 minutes or until all liquid is absorbed. Add parsley, lemon peel, and lemon juice. Toss lightly and serve hot.

4 to 6 servings

RICE SALAD

3¼ cups defatted chicken stock
½ cup brown rice
½ cup wild rice
1 bunch asparagus (about 1 pound),
tough stems removed
1 carrot
1 zucchini
1 stalk celery
1 small turnip or rutabaga
¼ cup rice vinegar
1 teaspoon Italian seasoning
Low-calorie sweetener to taste
1 jar (2 ounces) diced pimiento, drained

Combine chicken stock, brown rice, and wild rice in 2-quart saucepan. Cover and bring to a boil. Reduce heat and simmer 45 minutes or until all liquid is absorbed and rice is tender. Set aside to cool. Chop asparagus and cut carrot, zucchini, celery, and turnip in julienne strips. Place in steamer over simmering water, cover tightly, and steam until crisp-tender. Set aside to cool. Stir vegetables into rice. Combine vinegar, Italian seasoning, and sweetener, and pour over rice mixture. Add pimiento and toss lightly to combine. Spoon into serving dish, cover, and refrigerate until well chilled. Serve cold.

6 to 8 servings

HAWAIIAN SAUCE

Never Stik
1 green pepper, chopped
1 large onion, chopped
1 stalk celery, diced
2 cloves garlic, minced
1 firm banana, chopped
1 can (8 ounces) crushed pineapple in unsweetened
pineapple juice, undrained
1 can (8 ¾ ounces) peeled apricot halves,
chopped, liquid reserved
1 tablespoon lemon juice
1 teaspoon Chinese spice seasoning

Spray gourmet frying pan with Never Stik, and sauté green pepper, onion, celery, and garlic until tender. Add banana, pineapple and juice, apricots, reserved apricot liquid, and lemon juice. Mix well. Reduce heat, cover, and simmer until fruit is very soft. Add Chinese spice seasoning. Remove from heat and pour into container of blender or food processor. Process until smooth. Serve hot as sauce over chicken or fish. Store any leftover sauce in covered container in refrigerator.

about 3 cups

MELBA SAUCE

1 cup fresh or frozen berries (raspberries, blackberries,
strawberries, blueberries, etc.)
¼ cup low-calorie berry jam
1 tablespoon cornstarch
¼ teaspoon almond extract
Low-calorie sweetener to taste

Place berries in 1-quart saucepan. Combine jam, cornstarch, almond extract, and sweetener in small bowl and stir to combine. Stir into berries. Bring mixture to a boil. Remove from heat and set aside to cool slightly, stirring occasionally. Serve over poached fruit or Fruit Melba (page 67), or store in covered jar in refrigerator and warm before serving.

about 1 cup

APPLESAUCE

8 cooking apples, unpeeled, cut in chunks
1 can (6 ounces) apple juice concentrate, undiluted
½ teaspoon grated lemon peel
1 tablespoon lemon juice
2 teaspoons cinnamon
2 teaspoons nutmeg
1 teaspoon allspice
1 teaspoon ground cloves

Combine apples, apple juice concentrate, lemon peel, lemon juice, cinnamon, nutmeg, allspice, and cloves in Dutch oven. Cover and simmer until apples are tender. Set aside to cool slightly. Place apple mixture in container of blender or food processor and process until puréed. Refrigerate until well chilled before serving.

about 6 cups

FRUIT MELBA

6 apples, pears, peaches, nectarines, or any combination
of fresh fruit, peeled
½-inch cinnamon stick
1 clove
Melba Sauce (page 66)

Cut fruit in half and remove pits, cores, or seeds. Place fruit, cinnamon, and clove in 2-quart saucepan. Add ¼ inch water. Cover and simmer until fruit is just tender. Remove from heat and set aside to cool. Discard cinnamon and clove, drain off liquid, and serve fruit with Melba Sauce.

4 to 6 servings

Asparagus with Lemon Sauce (page 99), Sea Scallops in White Wine Sauce (page 90)

Chapter Three

Elegant
Entrées

BEEF BOURGUIGNONNE

1½ pounds boneless beef top loin steak
2 tablespoons butter or margarine
1 large onion, sliced
½ pound mushrooms, sliced
1 clove garlic, minced
1 cup dry red wine (Burgundy preferred)
½ cup beef broth, divided
¼ teaspoon marjoram
¼ teaspoon thyme
¼ teaspoon savory
½ teaspoon salt
¼ teaspoon freshly ground pepper
2 tablespoons all-purpose flour
Hot cooked egg noodles to serve (optional)

Trim excess fat from steak, cut in 1-inch cubes, and set aside.

Melt butter in Dutch oven over medium heat. Add onion, mushrooms, and garlic, and sauté until onion is transparent. Add steak and brown quickly on all sides. Reduce heat to low.

Add wine, ¼ cup beef broth, marjoram, thyme, savory, salt, and pepper. Cover and simmer 1 to 1½ hours or until beef is tender.

Place flour in small bowl. Stir in remaining ¼ cup beef broth until smooth. Stir flour mixture gradually into liquid in pan and cook until gravy is thickened.

Serve over noodles, if desired.

4 servings

POT ROAST WITH RED WINE GRAVY

1 beef chuck roast, boneless (about 2½ pounds)
1 onion, chopped
1 clove garlic, minced
1 can (16 ounces) stewed tomatoes
1 cup dry red wine
1 tablespoon Worcestershire sauce
1 envelope (1¼ ounces) onion soup mix
¼ cup firmly packed brown sugar
1 teaspoon Dijon-style mustard
½ teaspoon oregano
Salt and freshly ground pepper to taste
2 tablespoons cornstarch

Preheat oven to 325°F. Place roast in Dutch oven and sprinkle onion and garlic over roast. Combine tomatoes, wine, and Worcestershire in medium-size bowl and stir until well blended. Add onion soup mix, brown sugar, mustard, oregano, salt, and pepper. Stir until well blended. Pour over roast. Cover and bake 2 hours or until roast is tender.

Remove roast to serving platter. Combine 2 tablespoons water and cornstarch in small bowl. Stir until smooth. Add to gravy and stir until blended. Cook over medium heat until thickened. Serve with roast.

4 servings

STUFFED SEASONED FLANK STEAK

1 beef flank steak (about 1½ pounds)
½ cup chopped celery
2 green onions, chopped
2 cloves garlic, minced
1 tablespoon chopped fresh parsley
1 tablespoon butter or margarine, softened
1 cup seasoned croutons, crushed
¼ cup dry red wine
1 teaspoon Italian seasoning
1 tablespoon Worcestershire sauce
½ teaspoon salt
⅛ teaspoon freshly ground pepper

Pound beef to about ¼-inch thickness. Score both sides with tip of sharp knife and set aside.

Combine celery, green onions, garlic, and parsley in small bowl. Add butter and croutons and stir until well mixed.

Preheat oven to 325°F.

Spread stuffing over steak, leaving 1-inch border on all sides. Carefully roll up steak lengthwise and tie in 3 places with string. Combine wine, Italian seasoning, Worcestershire, salt, and pepper, and brush over steak. Place in Dutch oven. Cover and bake 1 hour.

Brush steak with pan drippings, turn over, and brush again. Bake 30 minutes or until tender.

4 to 6 servings

PAN-BROILED BEEF STEAKS

2 tablespoons clarified butter
2 beef loin tenderloin or rib eye steaks
⅛ teaspoon freshly ground pepper

Melt butter in gourmet frying pan over medium-high heat. Add steaks and sear both sides.

Sprinkle with pepper. Reduce heat to medium and cook to desired doneness, turning once or twice.

2 servings

Note: *To clarify butter, melt butter in 1-quart saucepan. Skim off foam and remove from heat. Let stand until milk solids settle on bottom of pan. Strain off clear liquid and discard residue. Refrigerate until ready to use. Use in any recipe that calls for clarified butter or a combination of butter and oil for frying. Clarified butter will not burn.*

STEAK DIANE

2 butterflied Pan-Broiled Beef Steaks (above)
2 green onions, chopped
2 tablespoons chopped fresh parsley
2 tablespoons ketchup
1 tablespoon steak sauce
1 teaspoon Dijon-style mustard
¼ cup cognac or brandy
Parsley sprigs and cherry tomatoes for garnish

Place hot Pan-Broiled Beef Steaks on warm heatproof serving platter. Cover and set aside.

Place green onions, parsley, ketchup, steak sauce, and mustard in hot frying pan, stir to combine, and cook over medium heat until mixture just comes to a boil. Add cognac. Remove from heat and light with match to flame.

Pour flaming sauce carefully over hot steaks. Garnish with parsley and decoratively trimmed tomatoes.

2 servings

(See photo page 75)

Menu:
Gourmet Dinner for Two

tossed green salad
Steak Diane (page 73)
Parslied New Potatoes (page 100)
Asparagus with Lemon Sauce (page 99)
fresh rolls and whipped butter
dry red wine
assorted fresh fruit and cheeses

Parslied New Potatoes (page 100), Steak Diane (page 73)

RAGOÛT DE BOEUF

2 pounds beef for stew, trimmed and cut in 1-inch cubes
1 teaspoon salt
½ teaspoon freshly ground pepper
3 to 4 tablespoons vegetable oil
1 clove garlic, minced
1½ cups beef broth, divided
1 cup dry red wine
¼ cup chopped fresh parsley
1 bay leaf
1 to 2 teaspoons Worcestershire sauce
10 small white onions
4 medium-size carrots, cut in 1½-inch chunks
2 medium-size potatoes, peeled and cut in 1-inch chunks
2 stalks celery, thickly sliced
¼ cup all-purpose flour

Season beef with salt and pepper. Heat oil in Dutch oven over medium heat. Add beef and brown on all sides. Add garlic and cook 2 minutes.

Add 1 cup beef broth, wine, parsley, bay leaf, and Worcestershire. Stir well, cover, and bring to a boil. Reduce heat to low. Add onions, carrots, potatoes, and celery. Cover and simmer 1½ hours or until meat and vegetables are tender.

Place flour in small bowl. Stir in remaining ½ cup beef broth slowly, stirring constantly until smooth. Pour into stew slowly, stirring, and cook until gravy is thickened. Discard bay leaf before serving.

4 servings

SAVORY LAMB RAGOÛT

2 tablespoons butter or margarine
2 tablespoons vegetable oil
2 pounds lamb for stew, trimmed and cut in 1-inch cubes
4 carrots, cut in chunks
4 medium-size potatoes, peeled and cut in chunks
2 stalks celery, cut in chunks
3½ cups beef broth, divided
1 teaspoon dillweed
1 teaspoon rosemary
1 bay leaf
Salt and freshly ground pepper to taste
1 package (10 ounces) frozen peas, thawed
¼ cup all-purpose flour

Heat butter and oil in Dutch oven over medium heat. Add lamb and brown on all sides. Add carrots, potatoes, celery, 3 cups beef broth, dillweed, rosemary, bay leaf, salt, and pepper. Cover and simmer 1 hour 15 minutes to 1 hour 30 minutes or until lamb is tender. Add peas.

   Place flour in small bowl. Stir in remaining ½ cup beef broth slowly, stirring constantly until smooth. Pour into stew slowly, stirring, and cook until gravy is thickened. Discard bay leaf before serving.

4 to 6 servings

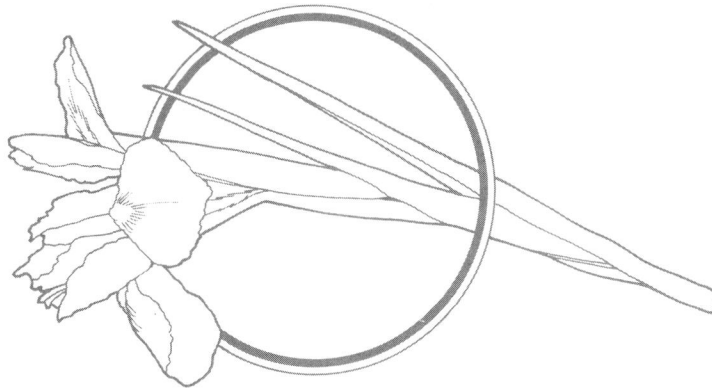

MINTED ORANGE LAMB CHOPS

4 lamb rib chops (3 to 4 ounces each)
1 tablespoon butter or margarine
1 teaspoon vegetable oil
Salt and lemon pepper to taste
2 tablespoons dry white wine
2 tablespoons orange juice
2 tablespoons mint jelly
1 tablespoon lime juice
Orange slices and chopped fresh mint leaves for garnish

Trim excess fat from chops. Heat butter and oil in gourmet frying pan over medium heat. Place chops in hot butter mixture. Sprinkle with salt and lemon pepper and brown chops on both sides. Drain off excess fat.

Add wine, orange juice, mint jelly, and lime juice, and stir well. Reduce heat to low. Cover and braise 15 minutes or to desired doneness.

Place on serving dish and garnish with orange slices and mint leaves.

2 servings

BUTTERFLIED LEG OF LAMB

1 clove garlic
1 boneless leg of lamb (3 to 4 pounds), butterflied
2 tablespoons soy sauce
2 teaspoons lemon juice
½ teaspoon thyme
½ teaspoon rosemary
½ teaspoon basil
¼ teaspoon freshly ground pepper
¼ cup vegetable oil

Preheat oven to 350°F. Cut garlic in half and rub over roast. Combine soy sauce, lemon juice, thyme, rosemary, basil, and pepper in small bowl and mix well. Brush over lamb. Roll roast and tie in 3 or 4 places with kitchen string.

Heat oil in Dutch oven. Add roast and brown on all sides over medium heat. Remove roast and drain off excess oil. Return roast to Dutch oven and bake 1½ to 2 hours or until internal temperature of roast reaches 135°F on meat thermometer for rare, 155°F for medium, or 165°F for well done. Let stand 10 to 15 minutes before slicing, to allow meat to set.

6 to 8 servings

PORK LOIN CHOPS IN CREAM SAUCE

2 to 3 tablespoons vegetable oil
4 pork loin chops, trimmed
3 green onions, sliced
½ pound mushrooms, sliced
1 large cooking apple, peeled, cored, and coarsely chopped
¼ cup dry white wine
¼ teaspoon basil
Salt and freshly ground pepper to taste
½ cup heavy cream
1 egg yolk, beaten

Heat oil in gourmet frying pan over medium heat. Brown pork chops on both sides. Drain off excess fat. Reduce heat and arrange green onions, mushrooms, and apple around chops.

Add wine, basil, salt, and pepper. Cover and cook 30 minutes or until pork is fork-tender. Remove chops to serving platter with slotted spoon and cover to keep warm.

Beat cream and egg yolk in small bowl. Pour into pan slowly and cook until thickened, stirring constantly. Serve over pork chops.

2 to 4 servings

PORK ROAST IN WINE SAUCE

¼ cup butter or margarine
1 boneless rolled pork loin roast (2 pounds)
1 large onion, sliced
1 pound mushrooms, thickly sliced
2 stalks celery, thinly sliced
1½ cups dry white wine
2 tablespoons cornstarch
3 large tomatoes, seeded and chopped
1 teaspoon Italian seasoning

Preheat oven to 300°F. Melt butter in Dutch oven over medium heat. Add roast and brown on all sides.

Arrange onion, mushrooms, celery, and wine around roast. Cover and bake 45 minutes.

Dissolve cornstarch in ½ cup cold water. Stir cornstarch mixture, tomatoes, and Italian seasoning into wine and vegetables. Cover and bake 15 minutes or until internal temperature of roast reaches 170°F on meat thermometer.

4 servings

VEAL CORDON BLEU

4 veal cutlets (about ½ pound)
¼ teaspoon freshly ground pepper
2 thick slices Swiss cheese (about 2 ounces)
2 slices thinly sliced cooked ham
1 egg, lightly beaten
1 to 2 tablespoons all-purpose flour
¼ to ½ cup seasoned dry bread crumbs
2 teaspoons butter or margarine
1 teaspoon vegetable oil
Chopped fresh parsley for garnish

Preheat oven to 375°F. Lightly pound cutlets. Sprinkle 2 cutlets with pepper. Place slice of cheese and ham on peppered cutlets. Brush edges with some of the egg. Top with remaining 2 cutlets and press edges to seal.

Coat cutlets with flour, dip in egg, and coat with bread crumbs.

Heat butter and oil in gourmet frying pan over medium heat. Add cutlets and cook 2 minutes on each side or until lightly browned. Drain off excess fat.

Bake 15 minutes. Remove pan from oven with hot pads and place cutlets on serving dish. Garnish with parsley.

2 servings

VEAL WITH HERBED SPINACH STUFFING

2 tablespoons butter or margarine
2 green onions, chopped
¼ pound mushrooms, chopped
¼ cup chopped celery
1 package (10 ounces) frozen chopped spinach, thawed
2 cups fresh bread crumbs
1 clove garlic, minced
1 teaspoon Italian seasoning
¼ teaspoon rosemary
Salt and freshly ground pepper to taste
1 boneless veal breast, cut with pocket (3 pounds)
1 cup chicken broth

Preheat oven to 350°F. Melt butter in 3-quart saucepan. Add green onions, mushrooms, and celery, and cook until tender. Squeeze spinach dry and add to saucepan. Add bread crumbs, garlic, Italian seasoning, rosemary, salt, and pepper. Stir well and simmer 1 or 2 minutes, stirring constantly.

Fill veal pocket with stuffing mixture and secure with wooden toothpicks. Place small wire rack in bottom of Dutch oven and pour chicken broth into pan. Add veal, cover, and bake 1 hour 30 minutes. Remove cover and bake 30 to 45 minutes or until meat thermometer inserted into thickest portion of meat reaches 175°F.

4 to 6 servings

ORIENTAL STIR-FRY

1 clove garlic, minced
¼ cup soy sauce
1 teaspoon lemon juice
1 teaspoon sugar
1 whole chicken breast (about 1 pound), split,
boned, skinned, and cut in strips
2 tablespoons vegetable oil
1 large carrot, thinly sliced
1 package (10 ounces) cut broccoli, thawed
1 package (6 ounces) frozen snow peas, thawed
½ cup sliced mushrooms
½ cup fresh bean sprouts
2 green onions, cut in 1-inch pieces
½ cup chicken broth
1 can (8 ounces) pineapple chunks, juice reserved
1 tablespoon cornstarch
½ teaspoon Chinese spice seasoning
Hot cooked rice or Chinese noodles to serve

Place garlic, soy sauce, lemon juice, and sugar in medium-size glass bowl and mix well. Add chicken and toss gently to coat with marinade. Cover and refrigerate 1 hour.

Preheat gourmet frying pan. Drain chicken, reserving marinade. Add oil and chicken to pan. Stir-fry over medium-high heat until lightly browned. Add carrot, broccoli, snow peas, and mushrooms. Stir-fry until vegetables are crisp-tender. Add bean sprouts and green onions. Stir-fry about 2 minutes.

Combine reserved marinade, chicken broth, pineapple juice, and cornstarch in small bowl. Stir until smooth. Gradually stir into chicken mixture. Add pineapple chunks and Chinese spice seasoning. Stir-fry until pineapple is heated through and broth has thickened.

Serve over rice.

4 servings

WINE-POACHED CHICKEN

4 whole chicken cutlets
½ teaspoon salt
¼ teaspoon lemon pepper
¼ to ½ cup chicken broth
¼ cup dry white wine
Creamy Mushroom Sauce (page 102), warmed
Chopped fresh parsley for garnish

Sprinkle chicken with salt and lemon pepper and place in gourmet frying pan. Add enough chicken broth and wine to cover chicken. Cover and simmer gently about 20 minutes or until chicken is fork-tender.

Remove from pan with slotted spoon and place on warm serving dish. Spoon mushroom sauce over chicken and garnish with parsley.

4 servings

CHICKEN AND WILD RICE

2 tablespoons butter or margarine
4 chicken cutlets
1 large onion, chopped
1 green or red pepper, chopped
1 can (16 ounces) stewed tomatoes
2 cups cooked wild rice
½ teaspoon Italian seasoning
Salt and freshly ground pepper to taste
½ cup (2 ounces) grated Monterey Jack cheese
½ teaspoon paprika

Melt butter in Dutch oven. Add chicken pieces and brown on all sides. Remove chicken with slotted spoon and set aside. Add onion and green pepper to pan and sauté until onion is transparent. Remove from heat.

Preheat oven to 350°F. Add tomatoes, rice, Italian seasoning, salt, and pepper to onion mixture and stir well. Place chicken over rice mixture and sprinkle cheese and paprika over top. Bake 15 to 20 minutes or until chicken is tender.

4 servings

Brandy-Glazed Chicken Roulades

BRANDY-GLAZED CHICKEN ROULADES

4 chicken cutlets
1 teaspoon salt
½ teaspoon lemon pepper
½ teaspoon chervil or thyme
2 tablespoons butter or margarine
¼ cup apple juice
1 tablespoon lemon juice
2 tablespoons honey
1 teaspoon cornstarch
¼ cup brandy
Sautéed apple slices and fresh thyme for garnish

Lightly pound chicken cutlets. Sprinkle salt, lemon pepper, and chervil over chicken. Roll up and secure with wooden toothpicks.

Melt butter in gourmet frying pan over medium heat. Add chicken and cook until browned on both sides.

Combine apple juice, lemon juice, and honey in small bowl. Stir until blended. Pour over chicken. Reduce heat to medium-low, cover, and cook until chicken is tender. Remove chicken rolls with slotted spoon and place on warm serving dish. Remove toothpicks, if desired. Place cornstarch in small bowl. Stir in brandy until smooth. Add to pan juices and cook until thickened. Pour over chicken rolls. Garnish with apple slices and thyme.

4 servings

TURKEY TETRAZZINI

½ cup butter or margarine, divided
2½ cups thinly sliced mushrooms (about ½ pound)
¼ cup all-purpose flour
2 cups chicken broth
½ cup heavy cream
1 egg yolk
3 cups diced cooked turkey
½ cup dry sherry
1 cup (4 ounces) grated Parmesan cheese, divided
2 teaspoons chopped fresh parsley
¼ teaspoon nutmeg (optional)
Salt and freshly ground pepper to taste
1 package (8 ounces) vermicelli, cooked

Melt ¼ cup butter in gourmet frying pan. Add mushrooms and sauté 5 minutes or until lightly browned. Set aside.

Melt remaining ¼ cup butter in Dutch oven. Add flour and cook 1 minute, stirring constantly. Pour in chicken broth and cream slowly and cook over low heat, stirring until slightly thickened. Beat egg yolk in small bowl. Slowly stir 4 tablespoons hot sauce into egg yolk. Pour egg yolk mixture back into sauce, stirring constantly. Simmer, stirring, 3 minutes. Add turkey, sherry, and ½ cup cheese. Stir well and cook until cheese melts and turkey is heated through. Stir in parsley, nutmeg, if desired, salt, and pepper.

Preheat oven to 350°F. Add mushrooms and vermicelli to turkey mixture and stir gently to mix well. Sprinkle with remaining ½ cup cheese. Place in oven and bake 10 minutes or until top is lightly browned.

6 servings

TURKEY AND BROCCOLI ROLL-UPS

4 large slices uncooked breast of turkey
(about 8 ounces)
1 package (10 ounces) frozen broccoli spears
2 teaspoons Dijon-style mustard
2 green onions, sliced
4 ounces Brie cheese, cut in quarters
2 to 4 tablespoons clarified butter (page 73)
or margarine
¼ cup (1 ounce) grated Parmesan cheese
1 cup White Sauce (page 102), warmed, to serve

Lightly pound turkey slices. Set aside. Cook broccoli spears in
2-quart saucepan according to package directions until just
tender. Drain and set aside.

Spread 1 side of each turkey slice with mustard and divide
broccoli spears and green onions evenly over mustard. Place Brie
cheese over broccoli. Roll up turkey slices and secure with wood-
en toothpicks.

Melt 2 tablespoons butter in gourmet frying pan over medium
heat. Place rolled turkey slices in hot butter. Turn to coat all
sides with butter. (Add additional butter if needed to prevent
sticking.) Cook until turkey is tender and browned.

Sprinkle with Parmesan cheese and serve with White Sauce.

2 to 4 servings

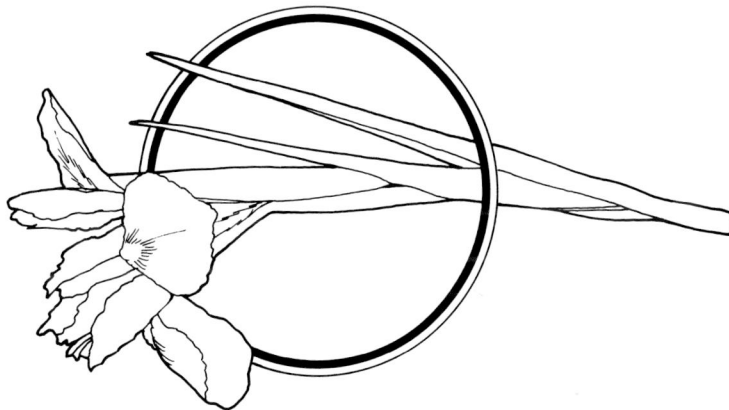

PAN FRIED FISH FILLETS

1½ pounds fish fillets
¾ cup crushed corn flakes
2 tablespoons chopped fresh parsley
1 green onion, chopped
½ teaspoon dillweed or tarragon
Salt and freshly ground pepper to taste
1 egg
2 tablespoons vegetable oil, divided
Lemon wedges to serve

Rinse fillets in cold water and pat dry. Combine corn flakes, parsley, green onion, dillweed, salt, and pepper. Place egg in shallow dish and beat lightly. Dip fillets in beaten egg, then roll in corn flake mixture, covering completely.

Heat 1 tablespoon oil in gourmet frying pan over medium heat. Add half the fish fillets and fry until fish are golden brown on both sides and flake easily with fork. Remove with slotted spatula and drain on paper towels. Add remaining 1 tablespoon oil to pan. Fry remaining fish fillets and drain.

Serve with lemon wedges.

4 servings

POACHED HALIBUT

4 halibut steaks (about 6 ounces each), cut 1 inch thick
¼ teaspoon tarragon or chervil
¼ teaspoon paprika
Salt and white pepper to taste
¼ cup dry white wine or chicken broth
Lemon wedges to serve

Season halibut with tarragon, paprika, salt, and pepper. Heat wine in gourmet frying pan. Place halibut in hot wine. Cover and simmer 10 minutes or until fish flakes easily with fork.

Serve with lemon wedges.

4 servings

JAMBALAYA

2 tablespoons butter or margarine
4 chicken cutlets, cut in half
1 cup diced cooked ham
1 clove garlic, minced
1 large onion, chopped
1 medium-size green pepper, chopped
1 stalk celery, chopped
1 can (16 ounces) stewed tomatoes
1½ cups chicken broth
½ teaspoon thyme
¼ teaspoon cayenne
2 bay leaves
½ pound medium-size shrimp, shelled and deveined
1 cup cooked rice
Salt and freshly ground pepper to taste
Chopped fresh parsley for garnish

Melt butter in Dutch oven over medium heat. Add chicken pieces
and brown on all sides. Remove chicken with slotted spoon and
set aside. Add ham, garlic, onion, green pepper, and celery to pan
and sauté until onion is transparent. Place tomatoes, chicken
broth, thyme, and cayenne in bowl and stir well. Add tomato
mixture and bay leaves to pan, cover, and bring to a boil. Add
chicken, shrimp, rice, salt, and pepper, and stir well. Cover and
simmer about 20 minutes or until chicken is tender. Remove bay
leaves and garnish with parsley before serving.

4 servings

SEA SCALLOPS IN WHITE WINE SAUCE

2 tablespoons butter or margarine
2 large cloves garlic, minced
2 green onions, chopped
⅛ teaspoon paprika
¼ cup dry white wine
1 tablespoon lemon juice
1 tablespoon olive or vegetable oil
½ pound sea scallops
¼ pound whole mushrooms, caps fluted
Chopped green onion for garnish

Combine butter, garlic, green onions, paprika, wine, and lemon juice in 1-quart saucepan. Cook over medium heat until mixture just comes to a boil. Remove from heat and cover to keep warm.

Preheat gourmet frying pan over medium heat. Add oil, scallops, and mushrooms, and sauté until scallops are white and mushrooms are tender, turning once. Add wine mixture and cook until just heated through. Spoon onto plates and garnish with green onion.

2 servings   (See photo page 68)

SHRIMP WITH FETTUCCINE

¼ cup butter or margarine
½ pound medium-size shrimp, shelled and deveined
1 clove garlic, minced
2 tablespoons chopped fresh chives
1 tablespoon all-purpose flour
¼ teaspoon basil
¼ teaspoon salt
¼ teaspoon freshly ground pepper
1 cup light cream or milk
1 package (8 ounces) fettuccine, cooked
2 tablespoons Parmesan cheese
1 tablespoon chopped fresh parsley for garnish

Melt butter in 2-quart saucepan over medium heat. Add shrimp and garlic and cook just until shrimp are pink. Sprinkle chives, flour, basil, salt, and pepper over shrimp. Stir well.

Gradually stir in cream and cook until sauce is thickened, stirring occasionally. Arrange hot fettuccine on serving platter. Spoon shrimp and sauce over fettuccine. Sprinkle with cheese and garnish with parsley.

2 servings

Note: *Cook fettuccine in 3-quart saucepan according to package directions. Drain and set aside, covered, to keep warm.*

LAKE TROUT JARDINIÈRE

2 trout (about 8 ounces each)
4 tablespoons butter or margarine, divided
6 mushrooms, sliced
1 green onion, chopped
2 tablespoons finely chopped celery
2 tablespoons grated carrots
Salt and freshly ground pepper to taste
2 tablespoons chopped fresh parsley for garnish
Lemon wedges to serve

Rinse trout in cold water and pat dry. Set aside. Melt 2 tablespoons butter in gourmet frying pan over medium heat. Add mushrooms, green onion, celery, carrots, salt, and pepper. Sauté over medium heat until tender. Remove from heat and divide mixture evenly in fish cavities. Season fish with salt and pepper.

Melt remaining 2 tablespoons butter in pan. Add fish and cook, turning once, until fish are brown and crispy and flake easily with fork.

Garnish with parsley and serve with lemon wedges.

2 servings

ROTELLE WITH VEGETABLES

1 tablespoon butter or margarine
1 tablespoon all-purpose flour
1 cup chicken broth
1 tablespoon lemon juice
1 clove garlic, minced
1 tablespoon chopped fresh parsley
½ teaspoon tarragon
Salt and freshly ground pepper to taste
2 medium-size carrots, cut in julienne strips
2 stalks celery, cut in julienne strips
2 small zucchini, cut in julienne strips
1 small sweet red onion, sliced and separated in rings
1 pound fresh rotelle pasta, cooked and drained

Melt butter in Dutch oven over medium heat. Add flour and stir until smooth. Cook 1 minute. Add chicken broth slowly, stirring constantly. Stir in lemon juice, garlic, parsley, tarragon, salt, and pepper. Add carrots and celery. Cover and cook 4 to 5 minutes or until vegetables are almost tender. Stir in zucchini and onion and cook 2 to 3 minutes.

Add pasta and stir until well mixed with vegetables. Cover and cook just until pasta is heated through.

4 servings

Note: *Fresh pasta is available in the refrigerated dairy department of your local supermarket.*

To cook 1 pound pasta, bring 3 quarts water to a rolling boil in Dutch oven over medium-high heat. Add 1 teaspoon oil, ½ teaspoon salt, and pasta, and cook 3 to 4 minutes or until tender.

SPINACH QUICHE

1 can (14 ounces) chopped spinach
Pastry for 1 unbaked 9-inch pie shell
½ pound sweet Italian sausage, crumbled, browned,
and drained
½ cup sliced mushrooms
1 medium-size onion, minced
1 clove garlic, minced
1 cup (4 ounces) ricotta cheese
1 cup (4 ounces) shredded mozzarella cheese
¼ cup (1 ounce) grated Parmesan cheese
4 eggs
1 cup evaporated milk
½ teaspoon Italian seasoning
Salt and freshly ground pepper to taste
1 tablespoon chopped fresh parsley
1 teaspoon chili powder

Preheat oven to 375°F. Squeeze spinach dry and set aside.

Press pastry into gourmet frying pan. Pinch edges. Spread sausage evenly over pie shell. Layer spinach, mushrooms, onion, garlic, and cheeses over sausage.

Combine eggs, milk, Italian seasoning, salt, and pepper in medium-size bowl and stir until well blended. Beat until frothy. Pour evenly over cheeses. Sprinkle parsley and chili powder over top of quiche.

Bake 45 to 50 minutes until center is set and tip of knife inserted in center comes out clean.

6 servings

*Green Beans Amandine (page 97), Harvard Beets (page 98),
Honey-Glazed Carrot Slivers (page 96)*

Chapter Four
Savory Sauces
and
Side Dishes

GREENGROCER'S MEDLEY

½ cup butter or margarine
1 medium-size onion, diced
1 small green pepper, diced
1 small sweet red pepper, diced
1 can (12 ounces) whole-kernel corn, drained
2 medium-size zucchini, sliced
1 can (6 ounces) sliced water chestnuts, drained
1 large tomato, seeded and coarsely chopped
¼ teaspoon basil
½ teaspoon salt
¼ teaspoon freshly ground pepper

Melt butter in gourmet frying pan over medium heat. Add onion and peppers, and sauté until onion is transparent.

Place peppers, corn, zucchini, water chestnuts, tomato, ¼ cup water, basil, salt, and pepper in 2-quart saucepan.

Cover and cook over medium heat until zucchini is tender. Drain off any excess liquid and spoon vegetables into serving dish.

6 servings

HONEY-GLAZED CARROT SLIVERS

1 pound carrots
3 tablespoons butter or margarine
3 tablespoons honey
½ teaspoon lime juice
Salt and freshly ground pepper to taste
Chopped fresh dill for garnish

Peel and trim carrots and cut diagonally into very thin slices. Melt butter in 3-quart saucepan over low heat. Add honey, lime juice, salt, and pepper, and stir. Add carrots, cover, and simmer, stirring occasionally, until carrots are tender and glazed.

Spoon carrots into warm serving dish and garnish with dill.

4 servings   *(See photo page 94)*

SAUTÉED MUSHROOM CAPS

¾ pound whole mushrooms
¼ cup butter or margarine
2 green onions, thinly sliced
1 clove garlic, minced
¼ cup dry white or Burgundy wine
Salt and freshly ground pepper to taste

Separate mushroom caps and stems. Refrigerate stems for use another time.

Melt butter in gourmet frying pan over medium heat. Add mushroom caps, green onions, and garlic, and sauté until mushrooms are tender, stirring occasionally to coat with butter.

Pour wine over mushrooms and season with salt and pepper. Stir until wine begins to bubble.

Serve with meat, over eggs or green beans, or as a flavorful side dish.

4 servings

GREEN BEANS AMANDINE

1 pound fresh green beans, trimmed
¼ cup butter or margarine
1 small sweet red pepper, cut in julienne strips
1 small yellow pepper, cut in julienne strips
½ cup sliced almonds
¼ teaspoon tarragon
Fresh tarragon sprig for garnish

Place beans in 3-quart saucepan and add lightly salted water to cover. Cook over medium heat until water comes to a boil. Reduce heat to medium-low. Cover and cook 10 minutes or until beans are tender. Drain well in colander and set aside.

Dry pan, add butter, and cook until melted. Add peppers, almonds, and tarragon, cover, and cook 3 to 4 minutes or until peppers are tender. Return beans to pan, stir well, and cook just until beans are heated through.

Garnish with sprig of tarragon.

4 servings (See photo page 94)

HARVARD BEETS

*1 can (16 ounces) diced, sliced, or small whole beets,
liquid reserved
Orange juice
1 tablespoon cornstarch
¼ cup sugar
¼ cup cider vinegar
½ teaspoon grated orange peel
½ teaspoon salt
⅛ teaspoon freshly ground pepper*

Pour beet liquid into 1-cup glass measure. Add enough orange juice to make 1 cup liquid.

Place cornstarch in small bowl, add ¼ cup liquid, and stir until smooth. Combine remaining liquid, sugar, vinegar, orange peel, salt, and pepper in 1-quart saucepan. Stir in cornstarch mixture. Cook over medium heat until mixture is thickened and clear, stirring occasionally.

Add beets and stir. Cover and cook until beets are heated through.

4 servings   *(See photo page 94)*

CORN-ON-THE-COB

*¼ cup milk
1 teaspoon sugar
6 ears fresh corn, husked and silked
Butter or margarine to serve
Salt and freshly ground pepper to serve*

Place 1 quart water in Dutch oven, add milk and sugar, cover, and bring to a full boil.

Reduce heat to medium, add corn, cover, and cook 5 minutes. Remove with tongs.

Serve hot with butter, salt, and pepper.

6 servings

Note: *Corn tastes best when it is cooked within a few hours of picking.*

CLASSIC RATATOUILLE

2 to 4 tablespoons olive oil
1 large onion, coarsely chopped
1 large green pepper, chopped
2 cloves garlic, minced
¾ pound zucchini, cut in chunks
1 pound eggplant, peeled and cut in chunks
¾ pound tomatoes, seeded and cut in chunks
½ teaspoon basil
½ teaspoon salt
¼ teaspoon freshly ground pepper
½ teaspoon thyme
¼ cup chopped fresh parsley
2 tablespoons grated Parmesan cheese

Preheat gourmet frying pan. Add oil, onion, green pepper, and garlic, and sauté 10 minutes or until onion is transparent. Add zucchini and eggplant and sauté until tender. Stir in tomatoes and seasonings.

Reduce heat to low, cover, and simmer 25 minutes, stirring occasionally. Spoon into serving dish and sprinkle with parsley and cheese before serving.

Serve hot or cover, refrigerate 4 to 6 hours or until chilled, and serve cold.

4 servings   *(See photo page 30)*

ASPARAGUS WITH LEMON SAUCE

1 pound fresh asparagus
Lemon Sauce (page 103), warmed
Lemon slices for garnish

Snap off tough ends of asparagus and trim ends so stalks fit in 3-quart saucepan. Add water to cover. Cover and cook over medium-high heat 8 to 10 minutes or until tender. Drain.

Arrange asparagus on warm serving platter. Pour Lemon Sauce over asparagus and garnish with lemon slices.

4 servings   *(See photo page 68)*

VERMICELLI SAUTÉ

¼ cup butter or margarine
2 or 3 green onions, sliced
1 clove garlic, minced
1 package (7 ounces) vermicelli, cooked
and well drained
¼ cup chopped fresh parsley
½ teaspoon celery salt
¼ teaspoon freshly ground pepper

Melt butter in gourmet frying pan over medium heat. Add green onions and garlic and sauté until green onions are tender. Add vermicelli, parsley, celery salt, and pepper, and sauté until lightly browned, stirring occasionally.

4 servings

PARSLIED NEW POTATOES

1 pound small potatoes, unpeeled
¼ cup butter or margarine
1 tablespoon minced fresh parsley
¼ teaspoon salt
⅛ teaspoon white pepper

Bring 1 quart lightly salted water to a boil in Dutch oven. Add potatoes, cover, and boil gently 20 to 30 minutes or until fork-tender. Drain in colander. Return to covered pan to keep warm. Using an orange zester, score potatoes crosswise and lengthwise, returning scored potatoes to covered pan.

Melt butter in 1-quart saucepan over medium heat. Stir parsley, salt, and pepper into butter. Place potatoes in warm serving dish. Pour butter mixture over potatoes and toss gently to coat.

4 servings *(See photo page 75)*

GOLDEN FRIED POTATOES

3 tablespoons butter or margarine
4 medium-size potatoes, peeled and sliced
1 medium-size onion, sliced
Salt and freshly ground pepper to taste

Melt butter in gourmet frying pan over medium heat. Add potatoes and onion. Cover and cook 15 minutes, stirring occasionally. Remove cover. Increase heat to medium-high and fry 10 minutes or until brown and crispy on bottom. Sprinkle with salt and pepper and turn out onto warm serving platter.

4 servings

MUSHROOM RISO

¼ cup butter or margarine
1 cup sliced mushrooms
1 small onion, chopped
1 clove garlic, minced
1½ cups chicken broth
1 cup long grain rice
½ cup dry white wine
2 eggs
¾ cup (3 ounces) grated Parmesan cheese
1 tablespoon chopped fresh parsley
Salt and freshly ground pepper to taste

Melt butter in 3-quart saucepan over medium-high heat. Add mushrooms, onion, and garlic, and sauté until onion is transparent. Add chicken broth.

Reduce heat to medium-low. Add rice and wine. Cover and cook 20 minutes or until all liquid is absorbed. Place eggs in small bowl and beat lightly. Stir small portion of rice mixture into eggs. Stir egg mixture back into rice.

Remove from heat and let stand, covered, 5 minutes. Add cheese, parsley, salt, and pepper, and toss lightly.

4 servings

CREAMY MUSHROOM SAUCE

3 tablespoons butter or margarine, melted
1½ cups sliced mushrooms (about ¼ pound)
3 green onions, chopped
2 tablespoons cornstarch
1½ cups chicken broth or dry white wine
Salt and freshly ground pepper to taste

Melt butter in 3-quart saucepan over medium heat. Add mushrooms and green onions and sauté until tender.

Place cornstarch in small bowl. Add chicken broth slowly and stir until smooth. Gradually stir into mushroom mixture and cook until sauce is thickened. Season with salt and pepper.

Serve warm over meat, vegetables, or omelets.

about 2¼ cups

WHITE SAUCE

2 tablespoons butter or margarine
2 tablespoons all-purpose flour
1 cup milk
¼ teaspoon salt
⅛ teaspoon white pepper

Melt butter in 1-quart saucepan over medium heat. Add flour and stir until smooth. Cook 1 minute. Add milk gradually, stirring constantly. Add salt and white pepper. Cook, stirring, until sauce is thickened.

1 cup

Note: *Stir ½ cup shredded cheese, 2 teaspoons chopped fresh herbs, or curry powder to taste into White Sauce for variety.*

MORNAY SAUCE

1½ tablespoons butter or margarine
1 tablespoon all-purpose flour
½ cup light cream
½ cup chicken broth
1 egg yolk
½ cup (2 ounces) shredded Swiss or Gruyère cheese
Salt and white pepper to taste

Melt butter in 1-quart saucepan over medium-low heat. Stir in flour until blended. Cook 1 minute. Gradually stir in cream and chicken broth and cook until slightly thickened, stirring constantly.

Place egg yolk in small bowl. Stir small portion of hot sauce into egg yolk. Return mixture to sauce and cook until thickened, stirring constantly. Stir in cheese, salt, and white pepper, and cook just until cheese melts.

about 1¼ cups

LEMON SAUCE

½ cup butter or margarine
⅓ cup lemon juice
1½ tablespoons grated lemon peel

Combine butter, lemon juice, and lemon peel in 1-quart saucepan. Cook over medium-high heat until mixture comes to a boil. Reduce heat to medium and cook 5 minutes, stirring occasionally.

Serve warm over vegetables.

about ½ cup

Note: *If desired, double recipe, chill, and serve cold over cake.*

Hot Alpine Cocoa (page 28), Blueberry Buttermilk Pancakes (page 53)

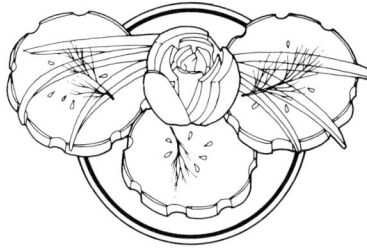

Menu:
Sunday Brunch for Eight

Hot Alpine Cocoa (page 28)
freshly squeezed orange juice
Blueberry Buttermilk Pancakes (page 53)
honey and maple syrup
Scrambled Eggs Manhattan-Style (page 51)
bran muffins with Rhubarb and Strawberry Preserves
(page 116)
pan fried link sausages

RHUBARB-PINEAPPLE SAUCE

4 cups diced rhubarb
1 cup sugar
1 can (16 ounces) pineapple chunks, juice reserved
1 tablespoon cornstarch
1 teaspoon lemon juice
1 teaspoon lime juice
1 orange, coarsely chopped
1 teaspoon vanilla

Combine rhubarb, sugar, and pineapple juice in Dutch oven. Stir until well mixed. Cook over medium heat until mixture comes to a boil, stirring occasionally. Continue to cook until rhubarb is tender.

Place cornstarch in small bowl and stir in lemon and lime juices until smooth. Combine pineapple chunks, orange, and cornstarch mixture in medium-size bowl. Stir into rhubarb mixture and cook until thickened, stirring occasionally. Add vanilla and stir.

Pour into container, cover, and refrigerate.

about 1 quart

HONEY LIME SAUCE

⅔ cup apple or pineapple juice
¼ cup honey
2 tablespoons lime juice
2 teaspoons cornstarch
1½ teaspoons celery seed

Combine apple juice, honey, lime juice, cornstarch, and celery seed in 1-quart saucepan. Stir until blended. Cook over medium-high heat until mixture comes to a boil.

Reduce heat to medium and boil until mixture coats a spoon, stirring constantly.

Serve warm with meat, or pour into covered container, refrigerate, and serve chilled with fruit.

about ½ cup

BUTTERSCOTCH SAUCE

1¼ cups firmly packed brown sugar
⅔ cup light corn syrup
¼ cup butter or margarine
⅔ cup light cream
1 teaspoon vanilla

Combine brown sugar, corn syrup, and butter in 2-quart saucepan. Stir until blended and smooth. Cook over medium-high heat until mixture comes to a boil, stirring occasionally.

Reduce heat to medium and cook until mixture coats a spoon, stirring constantly. Remove from heat and set aside to cool to room temperature. Stir in cream and vanilla. Pour into container, cover, and refrigerate.

To reheat, pour into 1-quart saucepan and cook over low heat until warm.

about 1½ cups

HOT FUDGE SAUCE

½ cup milk or light cream
1 cup semisweet chocolate morsels
1 cup sugar
2 tablespoons corn syrup
2 tablespoons butter or margarine
1 teaspoon vanilla
¼ teaspoon peppermint extract (optional)

Combine milk and chocolate morsels in 1-quart saucepan. Cook over medium heat until chocolate melts, stirring occasionally. Add sugar, corn syrup, and butter, and cook until mixture comes to a boil. Boil 10 minutes or until thick and glossy, stirring occasionally without touching sides of pan with spoon.

Remove from heat and stir in vanilla and peppermint extract, if desired. Cool to room temperature. Pour into covered container and refrigerate. To reheat, place in 1-quart saucepan and cook over low heat until just warm.

about 2 cups (See photo page 108)

Hot Fudge Sauce (page 107), Raisin Rum Sauce ,
Sweet Berry Sauce

SWEET BERRY SAUCE

¾ cup sugar
¼ cup lemon juice
1 pint raspberries
1 pint blueberries
1 tablespoon cornstarch
2 tablespoons butter or margarine

Combine sugar, ¼ cup water, and lemon juice in 3-quart sauce-pan. Cook over medium-high heat until mixture comes to a boil.

Reduce heat to medium. Add berries and stir. Cook until mixture returns to a boil, stirring occasionally.

Place cornstarch in small bowl. Add ¼ cup water and stir until smooth. Gradually stir into berries and cook until thickened, stirring constantly. Stir in butter until melted.

Serve warm as dessert topping or pour into covered container and refrigerate until ready to use.

about 3 cups

RAISIN RUM SAUCE

½ cup dark seedless raisins
½ cup currant or apple jelly
½ teaspoon coarsely grated lemon peel
¼ teaspoon cinnamon
½ cup apple juice
2 teaspoons cornstarch
2 tablespoons dark rum

Combine raisins and ½ cup water in 1-quart saucepan and cook over medium heat until mixture comes to a boil. Stir in jelly, lemon peel, and cinnamon, and stir.

Combine apple juice and cornstarch in small bowl and stir until smooth. Add to raisin mixture gradually and cook until thickened and clear, stirring occasionally. Remove from heat and stir in rum.

Serve warm over fruit or with ham or pork.

about 1½ cups

Bananas Foster (page 118)

Chapter Five

The
Confectionery
Shop

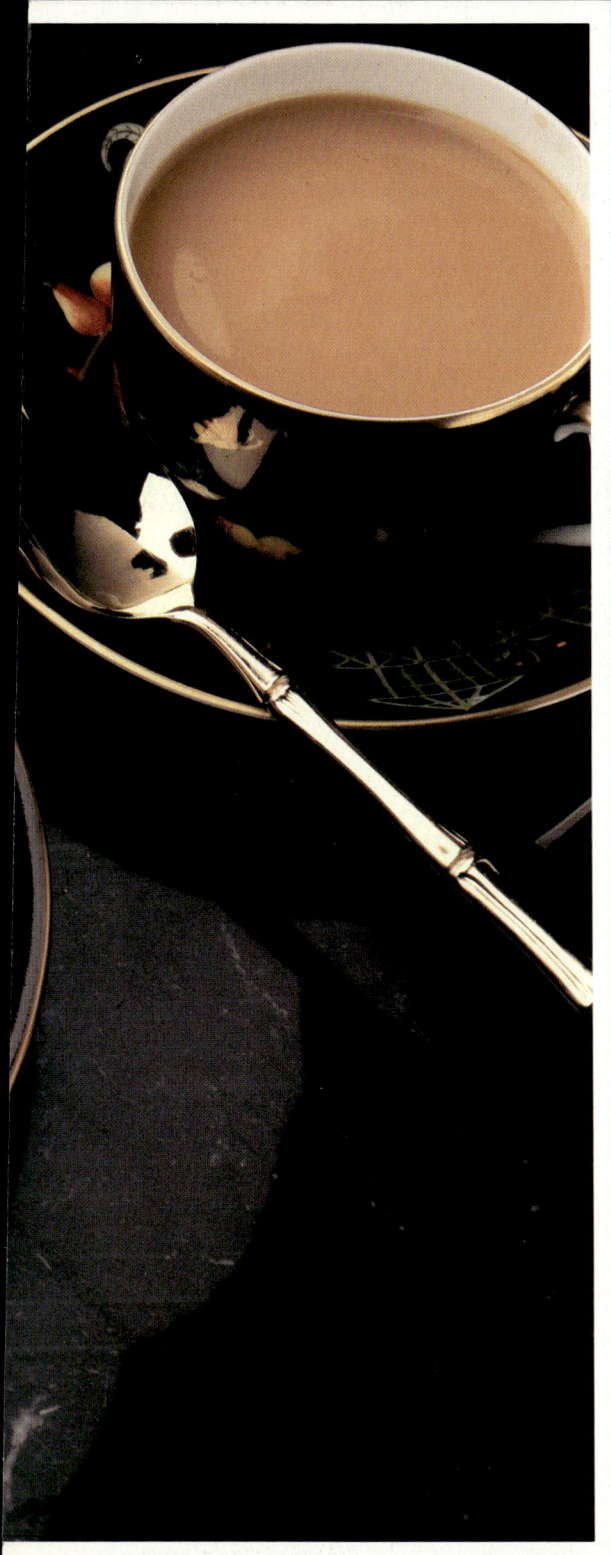

CHOCOLATE CHERRY CRÈME PIE

¼ cup butter or margarine
1 cup crisp rice cereal
½ cup all-purpose flour
¼ cup firmly packed brown sugar
1 package (6 ounces) chocolate pudding mix
1 can (12 ounces) evaporated milk
1 cup marshmallow crème
1 can (21 ounces) cherry pie filling

Preheat oven to 350°F. Melt butter in 1-quart saucepan over medium heat. Remove from heat and add cereal. Stir until well mixed. Add flour and brown sugar and stir. Press evenly onto bottom of 9-inch pie plate and bake 10 minutes. Cool completely on wire rack.

Combine pudding mix and milk in 3-quart saucepan. Cook over medium heat until thickened, stirring occasionally. Remove from heat and add marshmallow creme. Stir until blended. Fold in pie filling.

Pour into prepared crust. Refrigerate 2 to 4 hours or until set.

one 9-inch pie (6 to 8 servings)

FRENCH LACE PIE

½ cup milk chocolate morsels
1½ teaspoons vegetable shortening
1 baked 9-inch pie shell
1 package (3⅝ ounces) French vanilla pudding mix
1 can (12 ounces) evaporated milk
⅓ cup whole milk
1 cup shredded coconut
½ cup toasted sliced almonds
½ cup heavy cream, whipped, for garnish

Melt chocolate and shortening in 1-quart saucepan over low heat. Spread half the chocolate mixture over pie shell. Set remaining chocolate aside.

Combine pudding mix, evaporated milk, and whole milk in 2-quart saucepan. Cook over medium heat, stirring constantly, until thickened. Remove from heat and stir in coconut and almonds. Cover and refrigerate 30 minutes.

Spoon filling evenly into shell. Drizzle remaining chocolate mixture (reheat 1 to 2 minutes if set) over pie filling. Refrigerate 1 to 2 hours or until chilled. Pipe whipped cream around edge to make decorative border.

one 9-inch pie (8 servings)   *(See photo page 120)*

FRENCH PUFF PANCAKE (Clafouti)

⅔ cup all-purpose flour
⅓ cup granulated sugar
1½ teaspoons cinnamon, divided
¼ teaspoon nutmeg
¼ teaspoon grated lemon peel
¼ teaspoon salt
3 eggs, lightly beaten
1¼ cups milk
1 teaspoon vanilla
1 large cooking apple, peeled, cored, and sliced
½ cup confectioners sugar

Preheat oven to 350°F. Generously grease gourmet frying pan. Place flour, granulated sugar, 1 teaspoon cinnamon, nutmeg, lemon peel, and salt in medium-size bowl. Stir to combine. Add eggs and stir until smooth. Pour in milk slowly, stirring constantly, until smooth and well combined. Stir in vanilla.

Pour batter into prepared frying pan and arrange apple slices over batter. Bake 40 to 45 minutes or until tip of knife inserted in center comes out clean.

Slide out of pan onto warm serving platter. Sprinkle with confectioners sugar and remaining ½ teaspoon cinnamon.

6 servings

SCOTCH TORTE

CRUST
1⅓ cups graham cracker crumbs
¼ cup sugar
¼ cup butter or margarine, melted

FILLING
1 package (8 ounces) cream cheese, softened
¼ cup sugar
2 eggs
½ teaspoon vanilla

TOPPING
1 package (3⅝ ounces) butterscotch pudding mix
¼ cup firmly packed brown sugar
1 cup milk
1 can (16 ounces) pumpkin
1 teaspoon pumpkin pie spice
1 cup heavy cream, whipped, or 2 cups whipped dairy topping, divided

Preheat oven to 350°F. Grease 9-inch square cake pan.

To prepare crust, combine graham cracker crumbs, sugar, and butter, and press evenly onto bottom of prepared pan. Bake 5 minutes. Cool on wire rack before filling.

To prepare filling, place cream cheese and sugar in medium-size mixing bowl and beat until smooth. Add eggs, 1 at a time, beating well after each addition. Beat in vanilla. Pour into cooled crust and bake 20 minutes or until center is set. Cool on wire rack before adding topping.

To prepare topping, place pudding mix, brown sugar, and milk in 2-quart saucepan. Stir until blended. Cook over medium heat until thickened, stirring occasionally so mixture will not scorch. Stir in pumpkin and pumpkin pie spice. Spoon into medium-size bowl and refrigerate until almost set. Fold 1 cup whipped cream into pumpkin mixture until blended and fluffy. Spread over cooled filling.

Refrigerate at least 2 hours before serving. Cut in 9 squares and top each square with dollop of remaining 1 cup whipped cream.

one 9-inch torte (9 servings)

Cappuccino Fudge (page 123), Almond Bark (page 124), Scotch Torte

FRENCH CRÊPES

¼ cup all-purpose flour
1 tablespoon sugar
⅛ teaspoon salt
½ cup milk
2 eggs
4 tablespoons butter, melted, divided

Combine flour, sugar, and salt in small bowl. Add milk and eggs and stir until smooth. Cover and refrigerate 1 hour to set.

Preheat gourmet frying pan over medium-high heat. Stir 1½ tablespoons melted butter into crêpe batter. Brush frying pan with remaining melted butter. Remove frying pan from heat. Add 2 to 3 tablespoons crêpe batter and swirl pan to coat bottom. Pour out any excess batter. Return to heat and cook until bottom of crêpe is lightly browned and edges begin to dry. (Reduce heat to medium if crêpes are browning too quickly.) Flip crêpe over and cook 1 minute just until crêpe is brown. Turn crêpe out onto plate. Use immediately or place waxed paper between crêpes, over-wrap, and store in freezer until ready to use. Thaw completely before using.

8 crêpes

RHUBARB AND STRAWBERRY PRESERVES

4 cups sugar
3 cups sliced rhubarb
2 cups whole strawberries (about 1 pint)
1 can (8 ounces) crushed pineapple, undrained
2 or 3 drops red food coloring (optional)

Combine sugar, rhubarb, strawberries, and pineapple with juice in Dutch oven. Cook over medium-high heat, stirring constantly, until mixture comes to a boil and sugar is dissolved. Boil 10 minutes or until mixture reaches 220°F on candy thermometer. When mixture has thickened, remove from heat and skim off any foam. Stir in food coloring, if desired.

Ladle into hot sterilized jars, filling jars to ⅛ inch from top. Seal immediately.

about 2 pints

APPLE CRÊPES

⅓ cup butter or margarine
6 large cooking apples, peeled, cored, and coarsely
diced
½ to ¾ cup firmly packed brown sugar
1 teaspoon pumpkin pie spice
½ teaspoon cinnamon
1 to 2 tablespoons lemon juice
8 French Crêpes (page 116), warmed
Apple Glaze (below), warmed

Melt butter in 3-quart saucepan over medium-low heat. Add apples and toss gently to coat. Add brown sugar, pumpkin pie spice, and cinnamon. Cover and cook just until apples are fork-tender, stirring once or twice. (Don't overcook apples. They should retain their shape.) Stir in lemon juice.

Spoon apples onto crêpes and fold sides of crêpes over apples. Place crêpes, folded-side down, on warm serving platter. Spoon warm Apple Glaze evenly over crêpes.

8 crêpes

APPLE GLAZE

¼ cup butter or margarine
2 cups firmly packed brown sugar
1 cup apple juice
1½ teaspoons vanilla
1 teaspoon cinnamon

Melt butter in 1-quart saucepan over medium-high heat. Add brown sugar and apple juice. Cook until mixture comes to a boil. Reduce heat to medium and boil 10 minutes or until mixture coats a spoon.

Remove from heat. Add vanilla and cinnamon and stir until blended. Serve warm over Apple Crêpes (above).

about 2 cups

POACHED PEARS

1½ cups sugar
5 whole cloves
2 sticks cinnamon
2 cups cranberry or orange juice
2 cups dry or sweet white wine
¼ cup lemon juice
4 firm ripe pears (6 to 8 ounces each)

Combine sugar, cloves, cinnamon, cranberry juice, wine, and lemon juice in Dutch oven. Stir until blended. Cook over medium-high heat until mixture comes to a boil and sugar is dissolved.

Peel and core pears. Place in hot syrup. Reduce heat to medium-low. Cover and cook 20 minutes or until pears are tender.

Remove from heat and let stand 20 minutes. Remove pears from liquid with slotted spoon and place in individual serving dishes. Chill before serving.

4 servings

BANANAS FOSTER

2 tablespoons butter or margarine
¼ cup firmly packed brown sugar
¼ teaspoon nutmeg
2 large bananas, cut in half lengthwise
2 teaspoons lemon juice
⅓ cup rum or brandy

Melt butter in gourmet frying pan over medium heat. Add brown sugar and nutmeg and stir until sugar is dissolved. Arrange bananas, cut-side down, in pan. Sprinkle lemon juice over bananas. Cook until bananas are lightly browned, turning once.

Remove from heat. Pour rum over bananas and light with match to flame. Tip pan slightly so sauce runs to 1 side. Baste bananas with flaming sauce until flame dies.

Cut bananas in 1-inch pieces and serve with sauce over ice cream.

2 servings

(See photo page 110)

CHOCOLATE COFFEE CRÈME

1 tablespoon unflavored gelatin
½ cup light cream
¼ cup sugar
4 egg yolks
2 squares (1 ounce each) German sweet chocolate,
broken in pieces
1 to 2 tablespoons coffee-flavored liqueur
1 teaspoon vanilla
1 cup heavy cream, whipped
8 whole strawberries
1 square (1 ounce) semisweet chocolate

Place gelatin in small bowl. Add ¼ cup cold water and stir until smooth. Set aside. Scald light cream in 1-quart saucepan over medium-low heat. Beat sugar and egg yolks in medium-size bowl until blended. Gradually stir small portion of scalded cream into egg mixture. Stir back into remaining hot cream and cook until mixture begins to thicken. Add German sweet chocolate and stir until melted.

Remove from heat and add soaked gelatin. Stir until smooth. Add liqueur and vanilla and stir until blended.

Pour into medium-size bowl. Cover and refrigerate 1 hour or until almost set. Fold in whipped cream. Spoon into individual serving dishes and refrigerate until ready to serve.

Rinse strawberries and pat dry. (Don't remove stems.) Melt semisweet chocolate in 1-quart saucepan over low heat. Remove from heat. Dip strawberries in melted chocolate and place on waxed paper until chocolate is set. Garnish each serving with chocolate-dipped strawberry.

8 servings

Chocolate-Dipped Cherries (page 122), Hot Cranberry Wine (page 28), French Lace Pie (page 112)

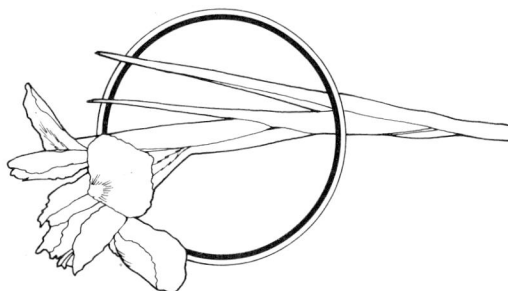

Menu:
After-the-Concert
Dessert & Coffee for Six

French Lace Pie (page 112)
Chocolate-Dipped Cherries (page 122)
Society Mints (page 124)
coffee
Hot Cranberry Wine (page 28)
assorted mixed nuts

CHOCOLATE-DIPPED CHERRIES

½ pound dark chocolate
1 teaspoon vegetable shortening
1 teaspoon Triple Sec
32 maraschino cherries with stems, drained

Place chocolate and shortening in 1-quart saucepan and cook over low heat until chocolate melts, stirring constantly. Remove from heat. Stir in Triple Sec.

Dip cherries in chocolate mixture and place on waxed paper until chocolate is set. Dipped cherries may be served immediately while chocolate is still warm or refrigerated and served chilled.

32 pieces

(See photo page 120)

ENGLISH TOFFEE

1 cup butter or margarine
¾ cup granulated sugar
¾ cup firmly packed brown sugar
1 cup pecan halves
1 teaspoon vanilla
½ teaspoon baking soda
½ cup milk chocolate morsels

Lightly grease jelly-roll pan. Melt butter in 3-quart saucepan over medium-high heat. Add granulated sugar, brown sugar, and 2 tablespoons water. Stir constantly until mixture comes to a boil. Reduce heat to medium. Continue to boil, stirring constantly without touching sides of pans with spoon, until mixture reaches 300°F on candy thermometer or small amount dropped into cold water forms hard crack.

Remove from heat and stir in pecans and vanilla. Add baking soda, stir, and pour quickly into prepared pan. Cool 5 minutes.

Sprinkle chocolate morsels over warm candy. As chocolate melts, spread evenly with metal spatula. Cool completely and break into pieces. Store in airtight containers.

about 1¼ pounds

CARAMEL NUT CANDY

1¼ pounds Light Caramels (page 125)
3 tablespoons milk
2 cups salted mixed nuts

Lightly grease 8-inch square pan. Combine caramels and milk in 2-quart saucepan and cook over medium-low heat until soft, stirring constantly. Remove from heat and stir through until caramels are smooth. Stir in nuts. Pour into prepared pan and set aside to cool completely. Cut in 1-inch squares. Store in airtight containers in cool place.

64 pieces

CAPPUCCINO FUDGE

3½ cups sugar
1 can (12 ounces) evaporated milk
4 squares (1 ounce each) unsweetened baking chocolate
½ cup butter or margarine
¼ cup light corn syrup
2 tablespoons instant cappuccino coffee
1 jar (7 ounces) whipped marshmallow topping
1 teaspoon rum or rum-flavored extract
½ cup chopped pistachio nuts

Grease 9-inch square pan. Combine sugar, milk, chocolate, butter, corn syrup, and cappuccino in Dutch oven. Cook over medium heat until chocolate melts and sugar is dissolved. (Don't stir down sides of pan because this will make fudge sugary.) Cook, stirring constantly, until mixture reaches 236°F on candy thermometer or small amount dropped into cold water forms soft ball. Set aside until mixture reaches room temperature.

Quickly stir in marshmallow topping, rum, and pistachio nuts. Spread in prepared pan. Cut in pieces when candy is set. Store in airtight containers.

about 2¼ pounds   *(See photo page 115)*

Variation: *For a more traditional fudge, eliminate cappuccino, substitute vanilla for rum, and use any kind of nuts desired.*

ALMOND BARK

1 cup blanched whole almonds
2 teaspoons butter or margarine
1 pound white chocolate, cut in small pieces
1 tablespoon vegetable shortening

Line baking sheet with lightly greased aluminum foil. Place almonds and butter in 1-quart saucepan and cook over medium heat until almonds are toasted, stirring occasionally to coat almonds with butter. Set aside.

Melt chocolate and shortening in 2-quart saucepan over medium-low heat, stirring constantly. Remove from heat and stir in almonds. Pour onto foil-lined baking sheet. Spread to desired thickness. Set aside to cool completely. Break in pieces when cool and store in airtight containers in cool place.

1½ pounds   *(See photo page 115)*

SOCIETY MINTS

2 cups sugar
¼ cup light corn syrup
¼ cup milk
¼ teaspoon cream of tartar
8 drops peppermint extract
Red, green, or yellow food coloring

Line 2 baking sheets with aluminum foil. Combine sugar, corn syrup, milk, and cream of tartar in 2-quart saucepan over medium-high heat until mixture comes to a boil, stirring constantly without touching sides of pan with spoon. Reduce heat to medium and continue to boil, without stirring, until mixture reaches 236°F on candy thermometer or small amount dropped into cold water forms soft ball. Remove from heat and cool slightly.

Beat vigorously until creamy. Add peppermint extract and food coloring. Drop by teaspoonfuls onto foil-lined baking sheets. Let stand until cool and firm. Store in airtight containers in cool place.

about 36 mints

LIGHT CARAMELS

1 cup sugar
1 cup dark corn syrup
½ cup butter or margarine
1 cup heavy cream, divided
1 teaspoon vanilla

Line 8-inch square pan with lightly greased aluminum foil. Combine sugar, corn syrup, butter, and ½ cup cream in 3-quart saucepan and cook over medium-high heat until mixture comes to a boil, stirring constantly. Reduce heat to medium and cook until mixture reaches 244°F on candy thermometer or small amount dropped into cold water forms firm ball.

Remove from heat and add remaining ½ cup cream gradually. Return to heat and cook until mixture again reaches 244°F on candy thermometer or small amount dropped into cold water forms firm ball. Remove from heat and stir in vanilla.

Quickly pour mixture into prepared pan. Set aside to cool completely. Remove from pan and cut in 1-inch squares. Store in airtight containers in cool place.

64 pieces

SWEET WALNUTS

½ cup sugar
½ teaspoon cinnamon
½ teaspoon pumpkin pie spice
¼ teaspoon salt
1 cup walnut halves

Line baking sheet with lightly greased aluminum foil. Combine sugar, ¼ cup water, cinnamon, pumpkin pie spice, and salt in 3-quart saucepan. Cook over medium-high heat until mixture comes to a boil. Continue to boil, stirring occasionally, until mixture reaches 236°F on candy thermometer, or small amount dropped into cold water forms soft ball. Remove from heat.

Stir in walnuts. Continue to stir a few minutes until creamy. Pour onto prepared baking sheet. Break apart when cool and store in airtight container.

about 2 cups

Index